Peterborough

History and Guide

Donald Mackreth

ALAN SUTTON PUBLISHING LIMITED

First published in the United Kingdom in 1994 by
Alan Sutton Publishing Ltd
Phoenix Mill · Far Thrupp · Stroud · Gloucestershire

First published in the United States of America in 1994 by
Alan Sutton Publishing Inc · 83 Washington Street · Dover · NH 03820

British Library Cataloguing in Publication Data

A catalogue record for this book is available from the British
Library.

ISBN 0–7509–0235–3

Library of Congress Cataloging in Publication Data applied for

Typeset in 10/13 Times.
Typesetting and origination by
Alan Sutton Publishing Limited.
Printed in Great Britain by
Redwood Books, Trowbridge, Wiltshire

Contents

CHAPTER ONE

Medeshamstede, the First Monastery and Before

T o Hugh Candidus, the first of the monk historians to write about the place we call Peterborough, there was no need to look for any reasons why the place was where it was. It was obvious. The edge of the Fens was so endowed with natural advantages that one would have to be an idiot to pass it by. The Fens themselves were:

valuable to men because therein are obtained in abundance all things that are needful that dwell nearby, logs and stubble for kindling, hay for feeding their beasts, thatch for roofing their houses, and many other things of use and profit, and what is more, it is very full of fish and fowl. There are many rivers and other waters and great fishponds. So this Burgh is built in a fair spot and goodly because on one side it is rich in fenland and on the other it has an abundance of ploughlands and woods with many fertile meadows and pastures. On all sides it is beautiful to look upon.

But a more modern approach is not satisfied with this: places do not just occur at random and why did Peterborough keep changing its name?

The wealth of the area in earlier times is reflected in the size of the Roman town of Durobrivae, and the number of villas in its neighbourhood, lying at the crossroads of the Roman equivalents of the A1 and A47. Here lay what was Roman Britain's Birmingham, and its pottery industry was, to a large extent, a kind of equivalent of that in eighteenth-century Staffordshire. To the west of the town was

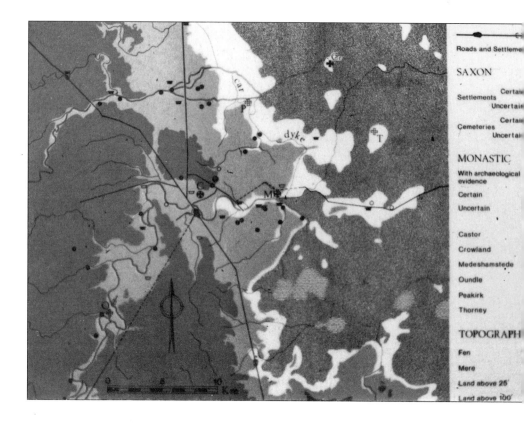

The area around
Medeshamstede (M) in S
times

one of the great iron producing areas in Roman Britain. Out to the
east lay the Fens, an enormous imperial estate run from a site
represented by the palace under the village of Castor, later to be
occupied by an Anglo-Saxon nunnery. All this, however, went the
way of Roman Britain at the end of the fourth and the beginning of
the fifth century. There are no records. All that can be seen is that
the economic strength began to wane and, somewhere about 425,
Anglo-Saxon settlers, possibly officially, were taking over Roman
sites. There is a scatter of Anglo-Saxon farm sites and cemeteries
around Peterborough, and a cluster of cemeteries towards the present
town centre may mark an important centre on the south bank, but
one now destroyed by the modern town and the brick pits.

All this evidence is archaeological, for there is no name to put to
any act here before the end of the sixth century. At this point there is
a set of records that is hard to place, but point to a second wave of
Anglo-Saxons. It is these people who provide the earliest names in
the history of the district. The suggestion of these records is that the
Mercian royal house only really came into being towards the end of

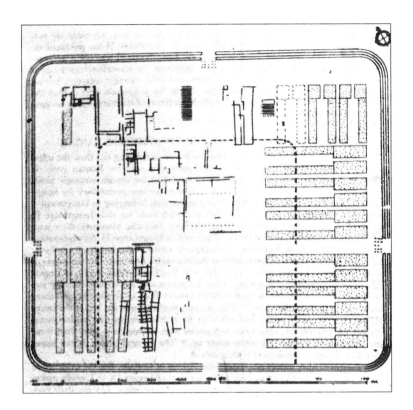

gthorpe Fortress, now
e golf-course

the sixth century when the family, having taken part in the earlier
sixth-century invasion of East Anglia, decided to move west with its
followers. The logic is that their route would have been through the
Peterborough region. At that time there was almost certainly no
visible distinction between inhabitants descended from Romano-
British natives and those descended from the first barbarian settlers.
Certainly there is nothing in the archaeology that is not Anglo-Saxon
and the new warriors who were to form the core of the Mercian
aristocracy would have been opposed only by people speaking their
tongue and living as they did.

The only record of the founding of the monastery here is in Bede's
History of the English Church, in which he says that Saxulf, the
constructor and Abbot of Medeshamstede, was made Bishop of
Mercia when Winfrid was deposed. The date of this event was about
674. The term *constructor* is usually translated as founder. We do not
have good evidence for the date of the actual foundation at all, but
local tradition in the twelfth century said that the monastery came
into being under King Peada. He was the son of the warlike and
pagan King Penda of Mercia, who thought it expedient that good

relations should be maintained with the most powerful kingdom, Northumbria. Although the limited records suggest that there was frequent war between the two, Penda sent his son Peada off to the north to get married. As the Northumbrian royal house was Christian, Peada had to be baptized before he could wed, and the royal pair returned with a missionary expedition. As the Northumbrian Church was at that time under Celtic influence, and the Celtic Church was organized around the monastic system, the missionaries would have needed to set up a monastery.

Saxon brooches from cemeteries just south of river

All this provides the background, but does not of itself explain why the first monastery in all Mercia was to be located on the north bank of the Nene where it flows into the Fens, but one can guess. In 652, two years before Peada became King of Mercia, he had been made King of the Middle Angles and, if his marriage was at this time, the missionaries would automatically have come to this part of the world. An analysis of the politics of the time suggests very strongly that Penda set up his son to guard this end of the kingdom against the kings of East Anglia, whose only effective land approach lay along the equivalent of the present A47, which ran to Whittlesey, at that time, on the north bank of the Nene. Therefore the logical place for Peada to have his chief residence was somewhere in the same area. Unfortunately we do not know where. The first monastery would also have acted as a kind of Chapel Royal, and so the king's hall should not have been far away. There are historically attested royal associations with Castor and Crowland, and it is more than likely that St Guthlac and his sister Pega, whose name is imprisoned in Peakirk, were of the blood royal. All this coupled with the redoubtable and politically astute St Wilfrid having his chief Mercian base at Oundle, where he died, suggests that this area was the core of the royal estates at that time.

We will never know precisely why the site where the cathedral stands was chosen, but there is a Roman site there and it does sit on rock. Roman sites were often chosen, partly emotionally because the conversion of the English was a result of a missionary expedition from Rome, and partly because Roman sites contained readily usable stone for churches in a land where there was no tradition of masonry and quarrying. The first church was built in re-used Roman materials from the beginning. Very little of it has been seen, but it was a sizable structure for its time. That it was handsomely decorated with sculpture is shown by the rare survival of pieces both in the cathedral and at St Margaret's, Fletton, whose chancel was being rebuilt when the last relics of the Late Saxon church were swept away in readiness for the nave of the new monastic church in the twelfth century.

Tradition in the medieval monastery had it that there had been two founders. The first was Peada, but he was, in simple terms, a failure as a king: he was murdered at the instigation of his Christian Northumbrian queen and ruled the rump of Mercia after the crushing defeat of his father who died in battle. The second was his brother, Wulfhere, an altogether more charismatic figure. He it was who booted out the Northumbrians and became the most powerful king in England; he may have been regarded as the second founder because of the added aura his name gave to the place. However, in 664 there was a famous debate among churchmen at the Synod of Whitby. The meeting was the result of rivalry between the Roman Church of St Augustine and the Celtic Church, which had been here since late Roman times. Ostensibly an argument about when Easter should be celebrated, it resulted in the defeat of the Celtic Church and an acknowledgement that there should only be one Church, ruled from centres at Canterbury and York. The initial mission to Mercia had of course been Celtic, as it had come from Northumbria, and it may be that Wulfhere was called upon to confirm the changes the Synod had brought about. He may have issued a charter, but the one that bears his name is a blatant twelfth-century forgery.

It is easy today to forget the character of the society in which all these people lived. It was fiercely loyal and very conscious of blood relationships. The Christian Church was a strange thing. It was recognized as a body in its own right, but there was nothing in the society that would allow the existence of what we would call a corporation, something in law that behaves like a person, but which does not die. The early monasteries were almost always founded by members of royal houses, so much so that Saxulf was very probably a relation of both Penda and Peada, and they could be bequeathed as though they were personal property. Wilfrid, when he was dying at Oundle in 709, appointed his successor to that monastery. More than that, if other monasteries were founded from a base they were counted as part of the family of that base. When Breedon on the Hill was founded, the document giving permission specified that the House was to be subordinate to Medeshamstede. It is a rare survival, but it does explain why some Houses exerted influence out of all proportion to their political clout. Repton became a royal burial church for Mercian kings, but it was subject to Medeshamstede, a detail carefully glossed over in Felix's *Life of St Guthlac*. Guthlac, when he wanted to become a monk, entered that house for his initial instruction, and the Fens to which he retired were not the deserted waste his early eighth-century biographer makes them out to have been. Both Medeshamstede and Ely held great sway there already.

We will never know the extent of the influence exerted from Medeshamstede, but some idea is given by the remains of records that survived into the twelfth century at Peterborough. These can be divided into two groups: those that date from before the death of Saxulf in 691, and those that are later. The first group refers specifically to Breedon on the Hill and Repton, while the second names Woking and Basingstoke, and possibly Hoo in Kent. The fact that records dealing with these places only survived at Peterborough is enough to show that the monastery was the Mother House. As for other members of the 'family' owing a kind of allegiance, Hugh Candidus tells us that the following places were founded from Medeshamstede: Hanbury in Staffordshire, Lizard, Shifnal and Wattlesborough in Shropshire, Costesford and Stretford, Brixworth, Swineshead, Bardney and Thorney as well as Lodeshale and Aethelhuniglond, which remain unidentified. To these must be added Castor, where there was a nunnery to which two of King Wulfhere's sisters retired.

Cuthbald was the successor of Saxulf from about 674 until after the death of Wilfrid in 709, but beyond him we only have a very hazy knowledge. Abbots Egbald, Pusa, Beonna, Coelred and Hedda are only names, and Egbald and Pusa may not have been abbots here at all. Hedda is usually counted as an Abbot of Medeshamstede, but all that can be said is that he was Abbot of Breedon, had been a monk at Medeshamstede and was counted as one of their men. His association with the carved stone in the cathedral, sometimes known as the 'Monks' Stone' is mistaken, as that was not carved until he had been long dead. Another abbot, Botwine, active from about 756 to somewhere between 779 and 789, has been identified from other records. He may have been succeeded by the Beonna mentioned above who is recorded up to about 805. Such a confused picture is all too typical of the history of Mercia in the Middle Saxon period.

The collapse of the kingdom, the depredations of the Danes and the final supremacy of Wessex all led to the destruction of what had probably been a fairly full written history of Mercia. The great Mercian ruler Offa signed documents at Medeshamstede showing that the place was on at least one of his circuits through his kingdom, and the relatively frequent appearance of Botwine and Beonna in witness lists is a good sign that the abbots of this house stood high in the councils of Mercia. The archaeology of the

Opposite: excavation in the
cloisters showing part of the
seventh-century church

Part of a late eighth to e
ninth-century frieze in S
Margaret's, Fletton

monastic church points to a major refurbishment between the first
building and the Late Saxon alterations, and it should be to this that
the carved stones already mentioned belonged. All, save the 'Monks'
Stone', were parts of buildings and all belong, like the stones at
Breedon on the Hill, to the most sophisticated carving to be found in
Middle Saxon England. There can be no doubt that the centre of the
style was Medeshamstede, and this reflects the wealth of illuminated
manuscripts and metalwork that is lost to us. The only object of this
period that can be seen now is the glass palm cup in the cathedral
treasury.

The period comes to an end in silence. When next Medeshamstede
appears in history it is about to change its name to Burh. The
popular story, given in the *Anglo-Saxon Chronicle* and by Hugh
Candidus is that the Danes passed through Medeshamstede in 870
and left it a smoking ruin littered with corpses. Unfortunately both
the sources saying this were written in the twelfth century and
cannot be taken as prime evidence. Indeed, Hugh Candidus himself
spotted the flaw in the story when he says that ancient privileges
were found in a hole in one of the ruined walls. This was an attempt
to explain how it was that this supposedly burnt-out wreck still had
documents dating from before the arrival of the Danes. The truth is
almost certainly less romantic and more mundane. The quality of
devotion in Middle Saxon times had decreased to such an extent that
many monasteries became houses of canons who were allowed to

ghth to early ninth-
sculpture of St
l in St Margaret's,

marry. King Alfred bewails the fact that scarce a priest could be found who could read. This is often put down to the effects of the Danish ravages, but it fits better with declining standards that had already been detected in the earlier eighth century, fifty years before the Danes made their first recorded visitation. When the Danes began to settle, the lands under their control were too large for them to settle completely and most of the Anglo-Saxon population remained. The Danes were great pragmatists and traders. They almost certainly used the remnants of Mercian organization for their own benefit and this would include diverting the profits of the wealthy, if debilitated, church to their own coffers. This would explain why documents were kept and, just as they appointed an Anglo-Saxon king for the parts of Mercia they were not settling, so they may well have kept an institution going that could be used, but could also enjoy the poverty that monastic vows enjoined upon those who swore them.

CHAPTER TWO

Burh, the Second Monastery and the First New Town

The Danes had a profound effect on eastern England, even if they cannot be detected archaeologically. To them we owe the origin of many of our towns and directly, as a result of their settlement, the old county system. Before the Danes began to impress themselves on monkish chroniclers, England effectively had no towns as we understand them. Because the Danes were an alien body within England, and in a minority in most areas, they maintained their military organization, which was based on centres that began to develop as towns proper. Places like the five boroughs (Lincoln, Derby, Nottingham, Leicester and Stamford) along with Bedford, Huntingdon and Northampton became county towns, save for Stamford. All had defences, being military strongpoints. Outside the Danelaw, Alfred's great reconstruction of Wessex was based upon the creation of similar defended places. Many had been Roman towns, but there were many that were also newly founded centres, most of which later become towns. In other words both the Danes and the English, as we may now call them, needed defended places to protect themselves from the other side.

Alfred died in 899, and it was left to his son Edward the Elder to carry English arms into the Danelaw and to subject it to the only surviving English monarchy. The once great Kingdom of Northumbria had collapsed in civil war by the time the Danes arrived in numbers, both Kent and Essex had disappeared as independent states when Mercia was the top kingdom and the East Anglian line came to an end with the killing of St Edmund. What happened in Mercia is obscure. The last independent ruler was

te eighth to early ninth-
y 'Monks' Stone' in the
ral

Aethelred, described as Lord of the Mercians, who married
Alfred's daughter, Aethelflaed. These two commanded one wing of
the attack on the Danelaw, Edward the Elder attacking from the
south while they moved in from the west. The year 917 was
momentous, beginning with Edward restoring the defences of
Towcester and, after he had quelled the storm the Danes raised
against him, ending with his being lord of all the Danish lands
south of the Welland. In 918 his widowed sister, Aethelflaed, Lady
of the Mercians, died leaving a daughter, and Edward formally
took Mercia into his own hands. The next year he moved up to
Stamford and Nottingham, and by 921 he had been acknowledged
lord of all England by all living there as well as in Wales and in
parts of Scotland.

The bearing this had upon the future of Medeshamstede was great.
Edward formally created the shires and so Medeshamstede began its
long association with Northampton. The shires were based upon
defensible towns, and a large county like Northamptonshire had
more than one, but the full local government system only became
apparent towards the end of the tenth century. All this has been
reconstructed from historical fragments, including some that seem
very unpromising. Let us look at Hugh Candidus's story of

St Aethelwold and the rebuilding of ruined Medeshamstede, once the greatest monastery in Mercia. Remember, Hugh was writing in the middle of the twelfth century and had only the haziest idea of what had happened even a hundred years before. His sources were bald chronicles, saints' lives and the memories and traditions of those around him. He knew only the feudal Norman state that had replaced the Late Saxon system.

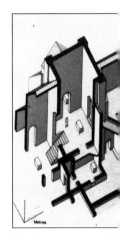

Imaginary reconstruction the tenth-century monast church

According to Hugh, Aethelwold was a mighty man of God who tirelessly set about restoring monasteries all over the place. One day God appeared to him and ordered him to go to a certain place in the lands of the Middle Angles and to rebuild a monastery dedicated to St Peter. Aethelwold left immediately and, arriving at Oundle, thought that this was the site and began work. But God appeared a second time and told him to move down river until he came to the walls of a burnt monastery. There he found cattle and sheep stalled in the church, and these he turned out to make the place clean. His resources were limited and he returned to Winchester where he prayed long and loud, so much so that the queen hid behind the door of the chapel to find out what the fuss was about. Needless to say, she persuaded the king to provide the funds and all was well.

The truth, as always, was much more complicated than that. We have seen that some remnant of the old monastery survived in a kind of working order. What St Aethelwold, along with St Dunstan, Archbishop of Canterbury, and St Oswald aimed to achieve was nothing less than the complete reform of the English Church. It was, in future, to be based upon monasteries, which would act as schools for churchmen and laymen alike. These were reformed according to the Rule of St Benedict and many were also cathedral monasteries. What is interesting is the scheme that seems to have been devised for the southern Danelaw, and this is where Oundle comes into the story. It had in Wilfrid's day belonged to a bishop of York. Before Aethelwold arrived on the scene it was almost certainly a possession of the archbishop of the same place, one dying and being buried there in the 950s. Now all the local reformed monasteries, save Ramsey, were ancient ones, and all were reformed by Aethelwold, except Ramsey, which was set up by Oswald, who happened to be Archbishop of York as well as being Bishop of Worcester. Basically the new scheme ended up with one monastery in each county. The kernel of this is present in Hugh's story about Oundle.

Where Danish influence was particularly strong the scheme could not be carried out to the letter. At this early stage there was no monastery in East Anglia, while the one in Lincolnshire, at Crowland, was very close to the southern border, and one proposed at Breedon on the Hill in Leicestershire failed to take off. A house of canons founded at Southwell in Nottinghamshire failed to develop into a monastery at all. Ramsey was in Huntingdonshire, Thorney in Cambridgeshire, Medeshamstede in Northamptonshire, and Ely may have been designed to serve East Anglia. More than that, the early abbots of Ramsey tended to become bishops of Dorchester on Thames, the precursor of the Diocese of Lincoln, and there is more than a suspicion that Medeshamstede was to provide archbishops of York. Like all schemes of this sort it broke down within a few generations.

One result of this administrative and clerical plan was that Medeshamstede changed its name to Burh, the first stage towards becoming Peterborough. The 'borough' part of the name has tended to be a puzzle to historians as it had nothing to do with mayors and councils, Peterborough having neither until 1874. The name was given in Late Saxon times when it could have only one meaning, that of a defended settlement, but this was strenuously denied by historians as Peterborough to them had plainly never had any defences. A burh, in English terms, was primarily what it had been for Alfred, for it was part of the defence of the kingdom and was normally controlled by a lord who was responsible for raising the military levies of the district. As it was important that it be occupied permanently, it was also a market centre and, because coinage was needed for that, it soon became customary for there to be a mint there as well. The problem with Peterborough was that although coins are known to have been minted in its name, the only reference in a document, admitted to be a forgery, said that the abbot could have the services of half a moneyer in Stamford. The Domesday Book, usually the best source for Late Saxon times, only mentions an agricultural settlement at Burh. All the evidence was seemingly stacked against there having been a real burh here.

In 1982 a trench was dug in the car park behind Peterscourt next to the precinct wall in the only place where that could be examined. The object was to see if the wall was early enough to have been part of the works of Abbot Martin de Bec in the middle of the twelfth century. The trench got deeper and deeper, and ended up in the fill of a medieval pond. At the point when the excavation was about to be closed, a broad band of stones and large lumps of a hard yellow mortar appeared. It proved to be the remains of a wall over 6 ft thick cut into the front of an earlier bank and, apparently, replacing a

Excavation of the late te
century burh wall in the
park next to Peterscourt

timber frontage. This was part of the northern burh wall. Re-
interpretation of what had been found in an earlier trench further east
behind the office block in Tout Hill Close showed that there was an
early ditch and a possible trace of a wall on the same alignment. A
trench later dug against the east precinct wall near its south end
revealed the last traces of a wall cut into an earlier bank, which itself
sat on top of dense Late Saxon occupation deposits. Two sides of the
burh have therefore been identified. They were in the logical place;

the walls would run round the Late Saxon monastery and not around the present town centre, which in any case is no earlier than the twelfth century.

One of the features of the Late Saxon state was that its organization was highly centralized and based upon the king's powers. It was this that enabled William to have the Domesday Book compiled, and it may be doubted if any other similarly sized state in Europe at the time could have achieved the same kind of thing. We know of Alfred's burhs through a document known as the Burghal Hidage. This attributes tracts of countryside to each one and has a set of computations showing that the size of the land was directly proportional to the length of wall. Now the abbot of the reformed monastery at Burh had jurisdiction over a quarter of Northamptonshire, the original Soke of Peterborough. This amounted to 800 hides, a hide being a fiscal unit, so the length of the burh wall can be calculated. In a nutshell, the southern defences run along the south side just north of the Almoner's Hall and the western side is not far in front of the west front of the cathedral. We now had the coins and the defences of a burh, but what about the market and the people?

One of the ways in which medieval kings raised extra cash was to delay the appointment of new abbots, so they could put in an administrator and take the profits that would normally have accrued to the incumbent. For two years from 1125 the king kept the abbacy here vacant, appointing Walter the Archdeacon as administrator. His accounts survive and they show something of great interest. He was here before the new town centre was laid out, so half of the double settlement revealed in his accounts cannot be mistaken for either the old agricultural settlement or the new town. What Walter describes is the Domesday village and a separate settlement, which was obviously the service town for the monastery.

The view that Domesday recorded absolutely everything is mistaken. The prime purpose of the record was to say what it was that belonged to the king in lands or taxes and what of these could be made to yield more. If the king had no chance of any income from something, it was not mentioned. The medieval town of Peterborough was absolutely in the ownership of the abbot: no one else, not even the king, owned any part of it. This is why the burh does not appear in Domesday. We now have a population, but where was the market? There was hardly room inside the walls, but a look at Eyre's survey of 1721 shows east of the precinct a vaguely trumpet-shaped area defined by roads, with its mouthpiece, so to speak, against the precinct wall by Vineyard House. This can only really be a market-place later divided into housing plots when its functions were either done away with or moved elsewhere – in the case of Peterborough to a new market-place on the other side of the monastery.

As a result of archaeological investigation, a look at medieval records and a piece of historical geography, the burh stands revealed, complete with market-place and agricultural community. We can say little enough about the inside as it is not available for excavation, but we can reconstruct the original monastic precinct as having been a rectangle with one side occupying the middle of the western side of the defences. At the same time that the trench was dug against the east precinct wall, another was laid out to test the interior of the burh, and dense occupation was found, with the remains of timber buildings and huge amounts of waste bone. The occupation all came to an end in the middle of the twelfth century, which fits the written history remarkably well.

Conjectural layout of the

The change of name can be dated fairly accurately. Hugh Candidus thought it was a result of the refoundation of the monastery by St Aethelwold, and that would have to be before 984 when he died. The *Anglo-Saxon Chronicle*, the Peterborough version compiled in the twelfth century, said that it was the result of Abbot Cenulf having put a wall round the monastery for the first time, and that would have been between 992 and 1005. In fact the real date is probably between 970 and 975 when the monastery and burh, with its earth and timber defences, came into being and Hugh was probably right to say the change in name was due to Aethelwold; after all, the inserted stone wall should be the one mentioned as having been built by Cenulf.

The first abbot of the reformed house was Ealdulf, said by Hugh to have been chancellor of King Edgar, the grandson of Edward the Elder. He occurs in what is known as the Peterborough Surety List, a document recording the careful securing of property in the name of the monastery dating basically from about 975 to 992. No particular tradition survived of his rule here and he later become Bishop of Worcester and Archbishop of York, holding the two posts simultaneously just as St Oswald his predecessor had done. He was succeeded at Peterborough by Cenulf, who was made Bishop of Winchester in 1005. His successor as abbot was the redoubtable Aelfsige, who controlled the monastery until 1042 – through all the trials of the period of war between the Danes and Aethelred II, from which Cnut emerged victorious.

athedral from the east,
1850

In an age when the collecting of holy bones, and complete bodies where possible, was a popular religious pursuit, Abbot Aelfsige excelled. We can never know how many relics he garnered, but he raided Castor and Ryhall and took away to Burh the bodies of the sainted Middle Saxons Cynebergha and Cynaswitha, sisters of King Wulfhere, and Tibba, a kinswoman. His monks were very proud of his greatest coup, although it does not put him in a good light. The abbot was obviously welcome at court, and when the pressure from the Danes proved too much Aethelred II sent his wife, Emma, abroad into Normandy and the Abbot of Peterborough went with her, probably as her private chaplain. They were away for three years during which time there was a local famine and Aelfsige was able to buy many relics for, as Hugh was proud to say, next to nothing. The greatest prize was the body of St Florentin of Bonneval with his shrine, but without his head. The monks parted with the saint for 500 pounds of silver so they could buy food. This shows not only the level of the abbot's charity, but also the wealth he was able to command despite the burden of the Danegeld and being in exile.

Aelfsige's sojourn abroad with the queen did him no harm as, when Aethelred II died, his widow promptly married the new king, Cnut.

At that time Peterborough was known for its scriptorium and for the illuminated manuscripts it produced. The master of the scriptorium, Earnwig, promised the future St Wulfstan, who was a pupil in the monastery, two manuscripts with capitals decorated in gold, but when Cnut and Emma came on a visit they were given to the king. Their quality was such that Cnut sent them as a present to the Holy Roman Emperor. However, and this was the point of the story, one at least returned in a roundabout way to the future saint, and that, of course, was a miracle. Aelfsige was succeeded by Abbot Earnwig, very probably the same man as the one in the story, who Hugh laments as a simple man devoted more to holy matters than to the property of his church.

Hugh says that Earnwig resigned unnecessarily in 1052, and Abbot Leofric was appointed by Edward the Confessor. Behind this story lies a tangled political scene. The king had managed to force into exile the overbearing Earl Godwin and his sons, including Harold who was to die at the Battle of Hastings, but they invaded England and the king had to welcome them back. Before the exile, East Anglia was run by the Godwin faction; afterwards it went to Earl Leofric of Mercia, husband of Lady Godiva of famous memory. When Earl Godwin and his family, to which Edward's wife belonged, were restored to power, East Anglia reverted to its previous rule. Earl Leofric's lands were then threatened and it was an expedient course to appoint a strong successor to the powerful fortress of Peterborough. Abbot Leofric was nephew of Earl Leofric and also had control of the monasteries of Burton on Trent, Ramsey, Thorney and Crowland. Edward was making sure that the eastern borders of Earl Leofric's sphere of influence were well protected. Leofric was loyal to the state and when Harold ordered levies to fight Duke William who had landed in the south, he led his men, probably the full complement of 200, and returned from the battle to die a fortnight later. How many local people lay dead and dying on the battlefield we have no idea. Hugh, in his innocence, tells us that for very grief scarce anyone could be found to bury Abbot Leofric. A more cynical age would say that the corpse was politically tainted. Nevertheless, he was buried and the monks elected a new abbot, Brand. They were in a quandary, however, as it was customary to have elections confirmed by the king, but should they send to William, still in the deep south, or to the acknowledged heir apparent, the Aetheling? They hedged their bets and sent Brand first to the Aetheling and second to William who was furious, but agreed to the appointment on the payment of a very stiff fine.

Now we come to what is perhaps the most famous episode in Peterborough's history. In it all manner of strands are drawn together. It concerns the Bishop of Durham, an ex-monk of Peterborough whose brother had been bishop before and had retired back to Peterborough; the Danes, in what was to be their last attempt to seize England; William I, and what he had to do to ensure future stability; and last but not least Hereward, later called 'the Wake'.

William, after defeating Harold, tried to run England as Edward had done before, but there was always the problem of what to do about the north. Matters came to a head in 1069 when the Danish king, Swein, landed in the north, which promptly rose in his favour. A party of William's men was burnt to death in the house of the Bishop of Durham. William went north and, in view of the gravity of the situation, decided on a scorched earth policy. He defeated Swein who promptly set sail, the Bishop of Durham with him, landed in the

Peterborough in 1721

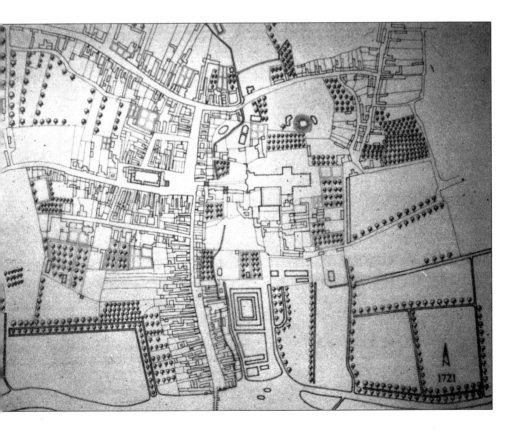

Wash and took over Ely. William had rebels behind him now and sent off reinforcements to his supporters in the south. Abbot Brand conveniently died at this moment and William sent the Abbot of Malmesbury, Torold, reputedly a ferocious man, as replacement along with a party of knights, either 120 or 160, depending on the manuscript. This is where Hereward comes in. He was a minor thane who held leases from the abbey, and who sided with the Danes when he scented profit. It was he who advised the Danes to mount a raid on Peterborough to remove its treasures before the new and warlike abbot arrived. The monks got wind of the intended raid and, knowing that Torold and the reinforcements had just arrived at Stamford, sent off a messenger with a few tokens to warn the new abbot of the threat. But that very day Hereward and the Danes arrived before the walls of Peterborough, which were fiercely defended by the abbey's men. This was the beginning of the battle of Bolhithe Gate, and the enemy only gained entry by starting a fire that burnt out most of the town and damaged the monastery. The site of the Bolhithe Gate was on the south side of the burh, where the later Bull Dyke lay, probably at the end of the path running south from the present cloisters. Hereward disappeared to become a hero of legend, and nothing else.

CHAPTER THREE

Burgh St Peter, the Second New Town

y the end of 1070 William had decided how he was to manage England. His men were too few on the ground to allow the old English state to run as before. He introduced the feudal system, which was based on a knight owing him military service in return for land. In order to find land he removed most of the previous English landowners and made sure that church lands were not exempt. The state was converted into a pyramid with the king at the top, every knight and lord swearing fealty in return for their lands. Peterborough was punished. Firstly, the two monks of Peterborough who had been Bishops of Durham were imprisoned, and secondly, a burden of sixty knights, the equivalent of a bishop's allotment, was imposed on the lands of the abbey. No other abbey was so encumbered, but as the Abbot of Bury St Edmunds had to provide for forty knights, and he was the king's friend, there was obviously a deeper reason for making eastern England strong: no one was to know that the Danes were never going to invade again.

There are signs that even sixteen years later the abbot was having difficulty in providing viable estates for all sixty knights. Only in name did the abbot become one of the most powerful of the king's men; in truth the king had crippled the economic power of this place and its lord. The burhs, relying as they did on the ordinary free fighting man to defend the walls, became obsolete overnight. The new power resided in castles, and one in earth and timber was built in the north-east corner of the old burh. Tout Hill at the bottom of the Dean's Garden is the mound on which the keep stood. There was now less room for the timber and clay town, with its thatched roofs, quickly rebuilt after the fire. The monastery was also repaired for, when Abbot Torold died twenty-eight years later, the chapter house had been begun, marking the start of a new layout. On the other hand, whatever good Torold did was quickly glossed over by the monks, who emphasized the impoverishment caused by his settling of knights on monastic land, ignoring the fact that Torold had to bow to the king's will.

The monks made one last attempt at ruling themselves. In 1099 they elected Godric, the brother of Brand, the last English abbot, paying William II 300 silver marks for the privilege. It did them no good, for in 1102 Godric was judged to have bought his office and was deposed along with the Abbots of Ely and Ramsey who had done the same. The woes of the monks were increased when robbers broke through one of the windows of the church and made off with practically all that had survived the thefts of Hereward and his friends. The robbers were caught, but William kept the treasure. The church had lost almost all its gold and silver and practically every relic, but was fortunate to recover the one that it prized most, the arm of the King of Northumbria, St Oswald, who died in battle against the pagan Penda in 642. William now provided an abbot much more to his liking, Matthew Ridel, who died exactly one year after being installed. The new king, Henry I, taking the abbot's income as profit, kept the abbey vacant until 1107, when he appointed Ernulf, Prior of Canterbury. Ernulf was much respected, principally for the benefits he brought the monks – among which were finishing the chapter house, building a new dormitory with its attendant latrines, and beginning the new refectory. In 1114 Ernulf was made Bishop of Rochester and, if what he achieved there is any guide, he left Peterborough with all its affairs in very good order.

All seemed set for an uneventful history in which abbot succeeded abbot. This settled picture was not to last, however. In 1116 the next abbot, John de Séez, finished the refectory, but it had been open for only three days when a major fire broke out. This started in the bakehouse and spread through the outer buildings of the monastery, destroying town and church, with the fire in the tower dedicated in 1059 lasting for nine days. The planned replacement for the buildings round the cloisters would have culminated in the provision of a new and grander church suitable for the sixty monks that the monastery housed. Now the abbot was forced to repair the old one immediately and took the decision straight away to begin a new church. This was to change the monastery and town out of all recognition.

The new church was planned to be twice as big as the old one, and when work began in 1118 the implications of this decision were not

…edral, the west side of
transept

obvious. Abbot John died in 1125 having laid out the east end and
built its lower two stages. The old church had been patched up for
use in the mean time, only the east end being completely demolished
to make room for the new building. Henry I kept the abbacy vacant
for two years, taking its profits, before appointing a kinsman, Henry
of Poitou, already Abbot of St Jean d'Angeli, who proved to be a
disaster. He was an acquisitive and duplicitous man who tried

23

several times to lay hands on a bishopric as well, but was foiled in his attempts. The *Peterborough Chronicle* says that he was given Peterborough in return for political favours, and Hugh Candidus gives details of how he tried to subject the monastery to the rule of that great monastic predator, the Abbey of Cluny. Ultimately he was ejected and was replaced by Martin de Bec, who proved to be a tower of strength in difficult times.

The reign of de Bec lasted from 1133 to 1155, almost exactly coinciding with the great turmoils of the mid-twelfth century known as the Anarchy, and its aftermath (1135–54). Henry I was succeeded by Stephen, but Henry's daughter Matilda, who was the widow of the Holy Roman Emperor, would have none of this and wanted the throne for her son. The Anarchy lasted from 1135 to 1148, but the last major military act was the capture of Stamford in 1153 by Matilda's son Henry Plantagenet, who was now Duke of Anjou and in control of Aquitaine through his immensely wealthy wife, Eleanor. In the same year Eustace, Stephen's son, died plundering the lands of the abbey of Bury St Edmunds, and Stephen acknowledged Henry to be his heir. The sixty knights of the Abbot of Peterborough ensured that the monastery was safe: no one wished to tangle with so great a lord. During this time the abbot continued building the church, bringing the east end into use in 1140. The demolition of the rest of the old church followed, the new nave being laid out over its remains right out to a new twin-towered west front, which was sited behind the present one. Laying out the plan showed up two main defects in the scheme: the great west door faced nothing but the back of the western defences of the burh only a few yards away, and the town lay behind the church. Abbot Martin decided to move the western boundary and the town.

The abbot could decide arbitrarily to move the town because he owned it lock, stock and barrel. Copies of a remarkable memorandum recording an impressive occasion survive. On 22 February 1145 at the beginning of the main mass of the day, before the high altar and in the presence of the relics of the saints, the abbot, the monks, the abbot's knights and the abbey's servants, two brothers surrendered all their rights in lands and houses once held by their father, Alsward. It just so happens we know about him. He appears in the accounts of Walter the Archdeacon as the only person other than the abbot who had rights in the old town, and they were leased to him in return for a range of duties. Abbot Martin was making sure that the sons did not try to claim a share in the new town.

front of the cathedral

These same accounts, prepared for the king when he took the abbot's profits between 1125 and 1127, provide a valuable picture of the people who lived in the town squashed into the south and east parts of the burh by the monastery and castle. In the church were two servants. The bakehouse had four bakers, a winnower and two carters, and attached to the bakehouse were two millers who had a servant. The brewery was run by one brewer served by two carters and three water carriers. The monks' kitchen had a master cook and one other, two wood carriers, a dish collector, an egg collector and a pottage maker. The tailor's workshop had two tailors, two men who washed cloths, a wood carrier and a cordwainer. There were three servants in the infirmary, and the work on the new church needed the services of two stone carters; the master mason was also on the payroll. The refectory servant, the pig-keeper and the courtyard keeper or porter come at the end of the list. This makes forty people, not including casual workers or the lay officers and servants of people like the almoner, the sacristan and cellarer, as well as the abbot's servants. Perhaps we can think of there being at least sixty people with wives and children all with houses inside the walls of the burh.

The problems of estimating minimum populations can be approached a different way. The same document talks of the people who lived 'in Burgo', which means in Burgh generally and not just inside the walls. First there is the agricultural community, made up of some fifty-nine unfree workers who all paid 45*s*. to the king. These are followed by others, clearly not serfs or villeins working in the fields, beginning with a group of fifty-five, then Alsward himself who held eighteen plots in tenancy and the unexplained 'theloneum de Hordesoca'. He is followed by ten servants who held by sergeancy, which means basically that they had land and houses to maintain them while carrying out the duties arising from their offices. These ten should not necessarily be numbered among the monastic servants already listed, but may have been the lay officers

Southern end of Broad Street with the iron Town Bridge in 1914

of the almoner, sacristan and the like. The knights of the abbey had eighteen lodgings, and there were six servants also with lodgings. In other words, somewhere between eighty and a hundred people had residences in the town.

The prime reason for moving the service town, as one might put it, was that the monastery needed more space. The church alone was to double in size and its principal entrance looked out on a rampart. Martin de Bec threw the west side of the Precincts across the stream just outside the old defences. This allowed his own quarters to expand enormously and be near the abbey's entrance, and also created a courtyard in front of the church, which could become the core of the business transactions between monastery and laity. The old town was flattened and its inhabitants were moved to a new site in front of the new Great Gate in Martin's new west wall. The water supply to the town was managed by diverting part of the stream on the west side of the old burh round the extended precinct. Parts of the bridge over it, joining the Great Gate and the Marketstead, as the Market Place in the town was called, now Cathedral Square, are still under the pavement.

The town now had a very large L-shaped Marketstead to replace the one on the other side of the monastery. The present Cathedral Square up to what is now Queen Street was one arm, while the other was Long Causeway, but there were then no buildings along the east side. This part joined with the street forming Westgate and Midgate, the latter known originally as Howegate. Long Causeway was really the north part of the main north–south street running down to a new hithe by the river, and the south part was, therefore, known as Hithegate: the bridge was built 160 years later. The other streets of the town were minor ones: Cowgate ran out to fields, Priestgate was the prime residential street with the houses on the south having gardens that overlooked the flood plain of the river, and Cumbergate was the small L-shaped street now subsumed into Queensgate. What is now Cross Street also belongs to the new plan. The term 'gate' has nothing to do with defences, but derives from the Danish word for 'way'.

The formal record of this activity is Hugh Candidus's crediting Martin de Bec with the laying out of the new gate to the monastery, the new Marketstead and the new hithe, these being the significant features of the new plan. A marginal addition to the continuation of Hugh Candidus's work also says that he destroyed the 'castellum'. This would at first sight appear to refer to the castle. Part of the treaty between Stephen and Henry seems to have been the agreement that 'adulterine' castles should be destroyed. However, the abbot's

Market day in Long Cau
in the late nineteenth cen

castle was legitimate, but even if it had lost most of its outer defences when the old burh was demolished the mound remained – a symbol of the abbot's right to have a castle. In the twelfth century the word castellum indicated a circuit of defences rather than something equipped with a keep, and the comment almost certainly refers to the burh's defences.

The abbot's court, which all the inhabitants of the old burh had to attend, was moved to the new gateway and the abbot's jail was established on the south side of that. It is as well to remember that no one had as much power within the Soke as the abbot; not even the king's officers were allowed to operate there. The abbot's court was very important to the townsfolk as it not only dealt with grievances, but was the place where all leases were renewed and all changes in sub-lettings between the abbot's tenants were approved, all for a fee of course. It is the loss of the court rolls that has deprived us of the detailed history of the town, its inhabitants and trades. We have to rely instead on individual charters, which could only be exchanged between free men and mainly concern the chief officers of the monastery, such as the almoner or sacristan. These can only give us hints, except for the one and only charter the town received before 1874.

Abbot Robert de Lindsey (1214–22) was on occasion embarrassed for cash, and one way of improving his income was to make concessions in return for greater rents. This is shown by his Charter of Liberties to the townsfolk. He put up all their rents by more than 150 per cent and in return they no longer had to pay an annual tallage, a fee when their daughters were married or for the licence when they did, and some of their agricultural duties were eased. They still had to attend the abbot's court and had to pay to use the abbot's communal oven. The abbot was keen to make sure that these extended privileges were not claimed by any Roger, Bill or Bob; he gave a list of tenancies and specified that only the named people were covered.

Among the 151 tenancies it can be seen that some properties had been divided into two, one or two had been amalgamated, and only one had had a complicated set of divisions. Such a 'pure' picture suits the relatively short period of about sixty or seventy years since the town had been newly laid out; any longer and the picture would be more confused. The document is straightforward, but the understanding of how the town actually 'worked' is not. The list was obviously taken from the abbot's rent-roll and can be run in order from the river, up the west side of Hithegate, later Bridge Street, then up and back again along Priestgate, back up Hithegate along the

south side of the Marketstead, up and down Cowgate, and round the west and north sides of the Marketstead, taking in the first leg of Cumbergate. From the south corner of Long Causeway, the list ran up to Westgate, taking in the second leg of Cumbergate, and finally along the south side of Westgate to cross over to the east corner of Lincoln Road, and to end opposite Wheel Yard.

The part of the town that best illustrates the relationships between the monastery and the people named in the Charter of Liberties is the section of Westgate running east from the junction with Lincoln Road, or Boroughbury as it was once better known. In the Charter we find that the corner plot is occupied by Alexander Carpenter, and then there is a set of plain names with little hint of who they may have been: Gilbert Curtgibet, Ascelin Suon, Gervase, Lambert de Norfolk, Thomas Osgot, William Winter and so on. Ascelin Suon may have been a member of the family of the abbot's hereditary pig-keeper, if not the man himself. We know from elsewhere that Thomas was son of Osgot and in turn had a son Henry, all of which tells us little more than we know of the rest. Individual charters can tell us a different story, and a group can be isolated that refers to the same corner and street frontage. We find that it is nearly all issued by the sacristan with the abbot's approval. His various tenants include a doctor and the family of a man who was fairly obviously a first-class embroiderer. The sacristan was responsible for the internal furnishing and decoration of the monastic church, and had control of a large budget. He was responsible for getting the windows glazed, the vaults painted, the church supplied with copes, candles and candlesticks, altar cloths, mass books and the hangings in the church. He had manors to provide the income and he employed people to do the work. These he settled on houses made available by the abbot and then these were sub-let to lesser mortals; it is these people who appear in the Charter of Liberties.

Without the survival of copies of a host of individual and apparently unimportant charters we would never have suspected the complexity of tenurial relationships to be found in the town. An illustration of the importance of being in a town and the hidden nature of some of the relationships lies in the presence of Robert, son of Robert Yol in the list of tenants. He began as a serf of Payne de Helpston, one of the abbot's knights. A serf was a piece of property, and he had no family in law. Payne gave Robert the father and his 'sequela', the nearest a serf could have to a proper family, to the abbot and returned the property down by the river which he had leased from the abbot, as well as the four pennies that Robert used to

ite: Robert de Lindsey's
ᴐ the Abbot's Lodging,
ᴂe Bishop's Palace

31

Thirteenth-century house
Goodyear's yard, off Nar
Street, as it was in the ear
twentieth century

pay Payne every year. In return he received from the abbot a gold
ring valued at one silver mark. A gentleman would not sell anything:
this was an exchange of gifts! But Robert, the son of a serf, by being
named in the list of tenants, became more free than all the serfs who
still lived at Helpston, or in Boongate just to the east of the
monastery, and more free than his father.

CHAPTER FOUR

Peterborough, Medieval Interlude

A bbot Martin was succeeded by William de Waterville, who was deposed in 1175, apparently because of the king's dislike of his brother's activities. An appeal to the Pope failed. William finished the great central tower of the church, which was rebuilt in the fourteenth century, possibly because of structural instability. The king kept the abbacy in his hands for two years and then appointed Benedict who, as Prior of Canterbury, had been responsible for the major rebuilding of Canterbury Cathedral. He continued the building at Peterborough with relish, and may even have brought one of the major glaziers, the so-called 'Methuselah Master', from Canterbury to work on glass for the windows. Although the monkish chronicles are not specific, it was he who decided to have a much grander west front than the twin-towered one that had been started, and he was almost certainly responsible for the first version of the three-arch scheme we see today.

Benedict was at Canterbury when Thomas à Becket was murdered, and brought various mementos with him to Peterborough. William de Waterville had already begun a chapel to the martyred archbishop; Benedict finished it and put the relics in its chancel. The chapel of St Thomas the Martyr stood on the north side of the Great Gate and straddled the precinct wall, the nave projecting into the market-place. The townsfolk naturally used the chapel for prayers, making offerings and tending to treat it like a parish church, which it was not, as that lay to the east of the monastery. This caused a dispute with the vicar and an arrangement had to be made in the chapter house to sort it out, but the matter was not finally settled until the early fifteenth century, when both the old church and the nave of the new chapel were pulled down to build the present parish church of St John the Baptist.

The next abbot who had a marked effect on the town was Godfrey de Crowland, instituted in 1299. The monastery had recovered from

The cathedral, the south-w
transept from the cloisters

the debts incurred by the heavy fines imposed on it by both sides during the civil war in Henry III's time, but both it and the town were saved from worse by the abbot's policy of keeping the monastery's doors open to both sides. Godfrey, apart from entertaining Edward II at great expense, was a great improver, and the chronicle of his reign really only gives a list of his works for each year, clearly abstracted straight from the abbot's accounts. However, two items are of great interest. In 1301 he spent the enormous sum of £25 on making, next to his private garden, a herbarium, which had the form of a moat within a moat with the necessary bridges. The moats survived to be put on the first good survey of the town in 1721. In 1307 he put a wall round his private garden, commonly known as the Derby Yard, and now the car park just south of the Bishop's Palace, as a prelude to improving his income from the town.

Until that wall was put up there had been no houses on the east side of Hithegate, and it was only after it had been built that the long rows between the river and the beginning of Howegate came into being. There had almost certainly been market stalls along the line backing against the precinct's wall previously, but these were now converted into proper shops with living accommodation – and appropriately increased rents. The houses north of the Great Gate were called Chapel Row, as they abutted the chapel of St Thomas the Martyr; those running south along the old precinct wall made up Sewtor, or Tailor, Row; and the last stretch against the Derby Yard and the herbarium down to the river was Rattan Row. The building of Sewtor Row converted what had been a broad street into a very constricted way known in later times, until the building of the present Town Hall, as Narrow Bridge Street.

Godfrey de Crowland's other major change was all of a piece with increasing the number of houses within what were fairly tight limits, and was the building of the first bridge. He did this in 1307, the same year that he made it possible to build the Rows, and he spent £14 8s. on it. This sum shows that it can only have been of wood and, as it was carried away by ice floes in the floods of that winter, it was replaced by a better and stronger one than the first at a cost of £18 5s., but it could still only have been of wood and the Town Bridge remained a wooden one until the end of the nineteenth century. Godfrey made it quite clear that although he had built the bridge the abbot and monastery were in no way responsible for repairing it or keeping it in good condition. As there was no town council or independent body in the town, who was going to be responsible was far from clear. What Godfrey almost certainly meant by this arrangement was that the bridge was not going to be a drain on the resources of the monastery: a replacement in stone on the orders of the king would be very expensive indeed: just to case the west side of the abbey's Great Gate and rebuild the upper parts took five years and cost Godfrey de Crowland £140.

The Town Bridge abou...

Almost all the main structures of the town were now in place, but four more features that completed the town as it was to be in the later Middle Ages need to be mentioned. The first of these is the church of St John the Baptist in the Marketstead. The other three were the provision of charities, the development of the major monastic granges and the appearance of major town houses.

The big event was the moving of the parish church. Apart from trouble between the vicar and the chaplain of the chapel of St Thomas the Martyr, the townsfolk made a general complaint that in winter it was awkward to get to the parish church along Howegate because of flooding at Martin's Bridge. This carried the road over the stream that divided to the south to flow through the Precincts and the town. We have no population figures, but the size of the new parish church suggests that a church, perhaps no bigger than the chapels at Paston, Longthorpe or Werrington, was inadequate. It was no easy matter to move a church, let alone amalgamate two. In 1402 a petition was sent to the Bishop of Lincoln and then on to the Pope with the result that permission was given to build a church more conveniently sited, and to demolish both the old parish church and the nave of St Thomas's chapel. While the new church was being built, the area of the old church where the font lay was to be kept roofed and marked by the cross on that side of town. The old cemetery was to be done away with, the ground being added to the

the Baptist's and the
ill in the middle of the
th century

almoner's land next to it, and the monks' cemetery on the north side
of the monastic church was to be used by the town. All the materials
from both church and chapel were to be used in the new building.
The abbot was William Genge (1396–1408), the first to wear a mitre
– which gave him the right to dedicate churches and chapels. Work
began in 1402 and he celebrated the first mass on 26 June 1407. The
first burial of an ordinary person, Lettice Goodbody, north of the
monastic church was on 7 July 1407.

The site chosen for the parish church was a prominent one in the
Marketstead, almost at the far end from the monastery, but not quite
because of the butchers' stalls. By long tradition these were at the
west end of the Marketstead and, while it may have been ancient
custom that left the butchers where they were, it is more likely that
ground frequently saturated with animal blood would not have been
considered fit for a church. As it was, the Marketstead was dug out
to cleanse the site, which is why the church sits in a hole in the
ground. This is a real hole, and not the result of the build-up of the
roads and buildings around.

Charity was a prescribed feature of monastic life, but it is not
always easy to see how it was provided. If one looks at the
straightforward accounts of income and expenditure prepared when

Henry VIII was planning to close down the major monasteries, the sums disbursed in the name of alms seem derisory. There are three aspects that need to be separated from each other. The alms mentioned in the accounts are extraordinary expenses and nothing to do with everyday charitable work. The most poorly documented part of this is the day-to-day duties of the almoner and his officers. It is true that the latter would be mainly concerned with maintaining the manors and other properties that formed the almoner's estate, the income from which was designed to support his work. Near the beginning of the 'Book of William Morton' (almoner from 1448 to 1462) there are calculations of how much wheat will yield how much flour, and how many 2 lb loaves can be baked from that. He finishes by telling us that, on the anniversary of the death (in 1295) of Abbot Richard of London, he distributed 858 loaves, each loaf weighing 2¼ pounds before baking. William Morton had a bake-house as part of his hall and was constantly baking bread for distribution, so this calculation was just an *aide-mémoire*: in his book he noted extraordinary expenses before writing them into his proper accounts.

In Robert de Lindsey's charter is a property named Hodierne, which does not have a tenant as such. It was just a name, the word being related to the Latin for 'today'. The property lay in the hands of the almoner who paid the abbot 16*d.* for it yearly. Analysis of the sacristan's rental of 1339–40 carried out by Tim Halliday shows that the house was on the north side of Priestgate towards the west end. By a charter dated roughly to the latter part of the eleventh century, Hugh, son of Stephen Cook, and his wife Paphet had given a property to the almoner for his use and for the poor. This is almost certainly the same property, but we are no wiser about the charitable uses to which it was put, unless this was the distribution centre for a daily dole of bread baked in the almoner's bakehouse.

By the end of the first quarter of the twelfth century Peterborough had a hospital, St Leonard's. This was for lepers, those suffering from deformities which aroused the greatest sense of horror among their fellow men. Nothing remains of it, but its site is commemorated by the Spital Bridge, which crosses the railway from Mayor's Walk to Westgate. The chapel in the hospital was dedicated to St Leonard and it was by his name that the institution became known. Gradually leprosy almost disappeared, and the hospital became an almshouse for old and infirm men under the management of the almoner. When the monastery was closed there were eight in residence. The almoner also had charge of an equivalent establishment known as the Sister

ecincts, the Almoner's
uilt about 1400

House, attached to the chapel of St Thomas the Martyr and paid for
out of the offerings made in the chapel. Provision was made here for
women and, like the men at St Leonard's, they attended services in
the chapel to pray for the souls of the founders. At the time it was
closed it catered for eight poor women. The monastic infirmary, more
like what we know as a hospital than the institutions called hospitals
in medieval times, was not open to the general public: the medical
man known to have lived in Westgate in the thirteenth century may
have dealt with the aches and pains of ordinary people.

The organization necessary to keep the monastery going was
considerable. Until the Black Death there were between sixty and
eighty monks. They had, as we have seen, a minimum of about forty
servants and there were several others who were attached to the
'offices' of the monastery. The abbot himself had a mighty
household, although we can never be sure how large it was on
average, and he would have had a minimum number of knights with
their servants in attendance as well. The people who did not toil in
the fields to produce the community's food could have numbered
over 150 at any time. The abbey was largely self-sufficient, relying
on its estates. The most important foodstuff was wheat, but we
should not forget the enormous quantities of barley needed to keep
the monastic brewhouse going. This food was stored in granges, of
which the most important was the abbot's located in Boroughbury,
the town end of Lincoln Road, named after the grange itself. The
sacristan had one, its name being corrupted to Sexton Barns, which

stood more or less where the main railway station is now. A third grange, called The Low, belonged to the infirmarer. As the only mass transport was by cart, these were constantly to be seen going through the town, and the 'Book of William Morton' is full of payments to carters for taking building materials to his various properties and for carrying bricks, bought in King's Lynn. Materials were brought by boat to the hithe by the Bull Dyke, just to the south of the Almoner's Hall, to be carted to his and other stores.

Town houses for the well-to-do were always at a premium, most of them being in the hands of officers of the Church. There are indications that Priestgate developed along its south side into a preferred residential area. Here the houses could have gardens running down to the flood plain, and could also be away from the more unpleasant smells of a town that did not have adequate drains or a sewerage system. We do know of one large house. It was built by Richard de Crowland, son of Benedict of Eye who married the sister of Godfrey de Crowland. He was a capable man and ended up with a lease on the ten properties running east from the junction of Lincoln Road with Westgate. By the time he died he had a hall and solar at one end, with a kitchen and a court entered by a gate in the middle and, at the east end, a building with a cellar under a solar. The site of this 'mansion' remained intact into the nineteenth century, when all was demolished to make way for North Street and the houses along it.

The political power arising from a close connection with the king's court, which the abbot had tended to enjoy, came to an end after the Black Death. The two were not connected, but that dreadful affliction marked a watershed for the whole kingdom. We do not know how many townsfolk died, but the enclosed life of the monk was almost ideal for the spread of the plague. Sixty-four are known to have died and, even with novices being made monks quickly, the community was reduced to thirty-two. Adam de Boothby (1320–38) was the last abbot who received members of the royal family and their entourages on a regular basis. In common with all lords, great attention was paid after the passing of the plague to ensure that the abbey got all it could from its estates: half the normal establishment of monks may have died, but there was no real let-up in the expenses of the House. The basic difficulty was that there were now fewer people working on the land. The appointment of a man to high office in the Church does not guarantee that he will be an excellent administrator, and there was a period of bad management in the fifteenth century culminating in Abbot Robert Kirkton (1497–1528), who liked to keep in his own hands various offices usually filled by

Opposite: the abbot's gre
barn in Boroughbury dur
demolition in 1892

40

Corner of Cumbergate an
Long Causeway about 19

monks – and it was not always certain what he had done with the money. He ran up against the mighty Cardinal Wolsey when he failed to pay the sums he had promised for the building of the cardinal's new college at Oxford. Kirkton was replaced by the cardinal's nominee, John Borough, also known as Chambers.

Abbot John was obviously an astute man and was grateful no doubt for having been awarded what looked like a rich and safe preferment, but in the 1530s the wind was blowing against the Church. Wolsey had not helped the king to secure from the Pope a divorce from Catherine of Aragon, and there were various other conflicts that suggested to Henry that the Church owed rather too much loyalty to the Pope for comfort. The king also had pressing money troubles, and curtailing the powers of the Church could address both problems.

CHAPTER FIVE

Cathedral and City: the First Steps

T he Dissolution of the Monasteries was the culmination of a series of events that arose from the fact that Henry VIII could not tolerate a foreign ruler, the Pope, having his own courts and a hierarchy whose first duty was to him and not to the king. The process now seems inexorable: the Pope was first denied payments, known as first fruits, made when an archbishop or bishop was appointed (1532), then Henry stopped all appeals to the Pope in legal cases (1533). This was followed by the king insisting that all new canon laws should be approved by a special commission, and finally that he should be acknowledged as Head of the Church, 'so far as the law of Christ would allow', in England (1534). Peterborough recognized Henry some months before it became a statutory obligation. The same year Henry had Parliament pass an Act whereby he got all the first fruits and tithes as well as spiritual tithes every Christmas. In 1535 various commissions were sent out to make a valuation of the Church's income so that the king could see what it was he should be getting. Thus was the scene set for the single biggest change in the ownership of land since the Norman Conquest.

A Commission visited Peterborough in 1535 and recorded a clear annual profit of £1,679 15s. 8¾d. from all estates and fees. The first blow against monasteries was actually administered by the Pope's representative in England, the formidable Cardinal Wolsey, who suppressed a series of small Houses so that he could use their lands to endow Cardinal College in Oxford, now known as Christ Church. This set a useful precedent, and in 1536 all Houses worth less than £200 a year were dissolved. The process gathered momentum, and in 1539 a new valuation stated that Peterborough was worth £1,979 7s. 5¾d. a year. In truth, the monastic ideal had waned considerably from the days when the endowments of the monastery enabled it to

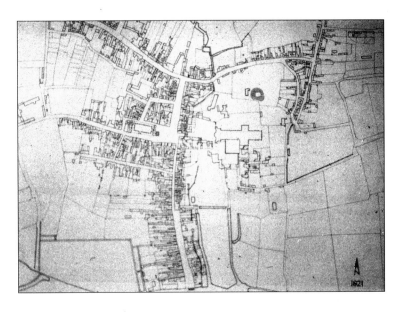

Map of Peterborough in

house first sixty and then eighty monks. The application of the Benedictine Rule had become weaker, with all sorts of privileges being regarded as rights. Many another House with a great tradition ceased to exist, but Peterborough was destined for other things. The local tradition that the burial of Henry's first wife, Catherine of Aragon, in January 1536 saved Peterborough is highly doubtful. The king is likely to have thought more deeply than that: the enormous Diocese of Lincoln needed to be trimmed to a more manageable size.

There was an interim period during which the ex-monastery became a college with the last abbot, John Chambers, as its warden and with a core staff, including a full choir of men and boys and an organist. There was also a new grammar school, the first version of the present King's School, whose statutes tell us that it was founded for twenty destitute boys without the help of friends. Nineteen ex-monks continued living in the Precincts with pensions, but the other sixteen, while receiving pensions, had to leave. Already the structure of the new organization that was to dominate the town until the setting up of a corporation was in embryo.

In 1541 the diocese and its cathedral became legal entities, and the town became a city with the right to return two Members of Parliament. The new diocese then consisted of Northamptonshire, Rutland and Leicestershire, the last being made a separate diocese in 1927. The warden was made the first bishop. In earlier days, when a man became a monk he gave up all connection with his family and was henceforth

nd of Broad Bridge
1 the late nineteenth

known only by a Christian name, sometimes with an addition to distinguish him from any other William, Robert or John. These extra names were always locative, taken from the places whence they had come. In the case of John Chambers we know that his other name was John Borough, which means that he was a native of Peterborough itself. The first dean, Francis Abree, or Leicester, was another displaced monk, this time the head of the priory of St Andrew's, Northampton. Twelve monks became the prebendaries and petty canons and the rest of the establishment was formally defined. One of the curious features of cathedral life in these times was that the petty canons, deacons and other officials, singing men, teachers, choristers and scholars were to dine together as a matter of course and were seated at three tables. The only roofed area not part of a dwelling or the cathedral itself big enough to accommodate them all was the nave of the infirmary, and it is perhaps significant that the prebendal dining room was attached to this. There were two cooks, one for the canons, and another for the rest who ate in the common hall. The cost of feeding the men and boys was provided from the income of the Dean and Chapter: a chorister for instance cost 10d. a week, but a petty canon or master was allowed 1s. 6d. a week. Like the petty canons and the rest, the scholars were provided with cloth for their gowns.

45

One of the difficulties that would have faced the king was that Peterborough had no independent body to run the town should the monastery disappear altogether. His policy here was to leave as much alone as possible. The former estates of the monastery were divided into three parts, one of which he kept, the other two being divided between the new bishop and the new Dean and Chapter. The king kept three-quarters of the jurisdiction the abbot had wielded, leaving the bishop with the rump, which became the Soke of Peterborough. The Dean and Chapter became lords of the manor, and their power here was as great as the abbot's had been, its last vestiges surviving until 1926. However, where the abbot's control had been tight and absolute, the new order was slacker. Its granting of unwise leases on the bishop's and the Dean and Chapter's estates brought both parties into trouble and ensured that Peterborough became one of the poorest cathedrals until the reforms in church finances in the middle of the last century.

The abbot had run four courts in the town and the double hundred of Nassaburgh. The major one was the court of quarter sessions for the double hundred and this passed to the bishop. Bishop Scambler surrendered his rights of jurisdiction to Elizabeth I, possibly because there was a suspicion that all was not well, but as the queen promptly granted the rights to Lord Burghley to whom the bishop had formerly been chaplain, one is entitled to smell a rat. Lord Burghley became Lord Paramount of Peterborough, a title still borne by the Marquis of Exeter, although all surviving power disappeared in 1965 when the Soke was amalgamated with Huntingdonshire. The Lord Paramount had his own jail, the Dean and Chapter maintaining another immediately south of the main gate into the precinct. The other three courts concerned the town alone and passed to the Dean and Chapter. The main one was the manor court, which was held twice a year. Everyone had to attend or pay a fine. The other two were the court of common pleas, held every week and the court of pie powder (derived from the Norman French for dusty feet, *pieds poudreux*) held on market days to deal with complaints.

As for the town, in the interim before the creation of the Dean and Chapter, the king had appointed Thomas Horseman as bailiff, and he remained in office when the new Dean and Chapter took over in 1541. He is last heard of when it is recorded that he had not settled a debt of £28 18*s.* 2*d.*, and he never did. No records tell us how the people of the town reacted to the change from abbot to Dean and Chapter, but it is more than likely that the removal of the strong

ates memorial, the
all and St John the
's about 1910

hand of the abbot gave rise to tensions between the governed and the governors. An indenture made in 1561 between the Dean and Chapter and fourteen men representing the town set out the customs regulating their relationship, and suggests the resolution of some kind of dispute. How the fourteen were chosen is not known, but six of them were to be members of the group of fourteen who formed the first Feoffees, of whom more anon. One purpose of the document was to confirm all the tenants, copyholders and freeholders in their properties for the time being and, so that there should be no mistake, a schedule of all such people and where they were in the town was attached to the document. Apart from the Rows against the precinct, the order of the schedule is the same as that in the list at the end of Robert de Lindsey's Charter of Liberties granted between 1214 and 1222. The list also shows that not only had the town hardly changed in the 350 years or so between the two documents, but also the abbot's rent roll was taken over lock, stock and barrel by the new lords of the manor.

A picture of the town as it was at this time survives in a draft record of the court held on 25 September 1538. Although this was before the Dissolution, what it has to tell us is repeated in another of 1544, showing that there was no significant change in the running of the town. The properties that had belonged to obedientiaries such as the sacristan, refectorer and almoner passed to new owners, but the rents had to be paid just the same. The town was divided into wards – Hithegate, Marketstead, Westgate, Priestgate and Boongate. The

Narrow Bridge Street in

first two wards had a constable, four decennerios and two beer tasters, while the remaining three had a constable and two decennerios. A decennerio ostensibly represented ten households and answered for their good behaviour, but the number of these men for each ward became fixed and, therefore, no longer gives a good indication of population. Their first business was to appoint new office-holders out of those eligible to serve on a jury. There was no election: the abbot, later the Dean and Chapter, chose from a shortlist submitted by the ward.

The job of beer taster was very important. We tend to forget that there was no tea or coffee, the water was often suspect and very few could afford wine. Beer was the everyday drink, being largely brewed outside the home, and nine brewers in the Marketstead are listed, as well as eight notorious drunkards. The quality of beer was a constant complaint and the tasters' business was to see that quality was maintained, brewers being fined if they sold any ale before its goodness had been assessed. Complaints were also laid against butchers who kept their meat until it was maggoty and against fishmongers who did not season their fish properly. The court roll tells us that the celebrated grave-digger Robert Scarlet lived in the Marketstead at that time. He was still there in 1561, only one queen having been buried by him at that stage.

The court rolls tell us an enormous amount about life in the new city. The draft of an early one just mentioned shows that freehold properties were now to be found in the town, there being at least twenty-eight of them. The courts were the places where deaths of householders were reported, inquests being held to see who were the rightful heirs and who had taken up new leases, as well as where affrays, theft and gambling houses (four cases) were dealt with. Another court roll, for 24 September 1544, shows the same number of wards, constables and decennarios. Attendance at the courts was obligatory. Several people did not come, claiming that, as they lived in the Precincts, they need not attend: they were fined. No one was spared. In 1570 the Earl of Bedford was fined 2*d.* for not attending as a freeholder. The complaints in 1544 were very much the same as before, with frays and the defying of constables well to the fore. Margaret and Katherine Toche paid a fee to the Dean and Chapter so that they could take up the tenancy of their late father Robert. The whole court yielded £9 4*s.* 10*d.* to the lords of the manor.

The major event in the history of the town in the latter part of the sixteenth century was the setting up of a body known as the

House in the middle of the
south side of Priestgate

Feoffees, of whom more below. At the time it must have seemed
pretty small beer, but from this small beginning came the
development of some of the aspects of organized city life, the
lighting and paving of the streets and the maintenance of public
wells, duties normally carried out by an elected corporation. The
dissolution of the monastery not only changed the charitable base

run by that institution (the two hospitals being replaced by the king's eight bedesmen) but the other feature of ordinary life, the charitable guild, a free association of men sanctioned by religious observances, had disappeared by 1547. These provided yet more land and income for the state, but at least one gift to the religious guilds in the parish church had a clause stating that if it were to decay the land in Cumbergate would go to the churchwardens. This, and other documents like it, passed into the hands of the Feoffees, which suggests that there was a close connection between them and these earlier guilds. An interesting detail is that the indenture drawn up in 1561 applied to the heirs and assignees of fourteen named men and, as six of them appear in the fourteen first Feoffees, it looks as though the group that became known as the Feoffees was already in existence.

There is an undated petition to Elizabeth I in which unnamed people in the town ask for some relief from various distresses, which shows that the loss of charity occasioned by the closing down of the monastery and the confiscation of the guild lands was deeply felt. The state sold the guild lands twice over within a few days in the latter part of 1571 to speculators. So that the townspeople could, through representatives, get the lands back, both sets of speculators had to be bought off. Three citizens, Thomas Robinson alias Baker, a victualler, Jeremy Green a haberdasher, and Robert Mallory, the farmer of tithes, bought the lands, and it seems that the three acted together to let the lands for profit to be used in charitable works, and to recoup their expenses. Mallory died early in 1572 and in June of that year the remaining two, the Feoffors, transferred the lands to fourteen men who, by this act, became Feoffees. Robinson was to receive £25 and Green £100 by instalments, the rest of the income being used to support the ten poorest people in the town, and any balance being devoted to mending the common ways on the north side of the river. This was the spring for all the other duties the Feoffees acquired during many reforms.

The Feoffees leased a property in Cumbergate to the Dean and Chapter to be a House of Correction, and by the early seventeenth century had two bailiffs and a beadle whose duty it was to administer the poor law. The Dean and Chapter, it must be admitted, saw the town mainly as a source of profit, their own duties lying in altogether other directions. The Feoffees ran some market stalls in the Butter Cross, where the Guildhall stands today, and also paid for works at the parish church (selling the wood from the spire in 1614), put orphans in apprenticeships and elected the churchwardens. In

times of plague the Feoffees provided a pesthouse, a kind of isolation hospital. How necessary such a thing was can be culled from records of the plague of 1665 in which it seems that over 450 people died. By the time of the Commonwealth this body, which was self-perpetuating, had virtually taken over all the main civic duties that any ordinary corporation would have. What is surprising is that the Feoffees should have maintained the weights and measures in the market when the bulk of the dues went to the abbot's successors. They also undertook fire-watching duties and the repair of the bridge for which the abbot had refused responsibility.

Education was not provided as a matter of course. The King's School, although for poor boys nominated by the Dean and Chapter, naturally catered for the sons of the clergymen, but none was to be admitted before he could read and write and knew the rudiments of grammar. Choristers were also admitted, but their musical education lay in the hands of a teacher appointed by the Dean and Chapter, who may or may not have been the organist. They were to be taught

Seventeenth to early nineteenth-century ho the south side of the Marketstead

King's School: the
ster's house on the left
boarding houses, built
cond quarter of the
th century

to play the viols and to sing. The scholars were to attend the main
services of the cathedral and swelled the choir on high days. The
original school rooms were the chancel of the chapel of St Thomas
the Martyr, just inside the Great Gate into the Precincts, and the
chapel of St Nicholas over the same gate. Education for others in
the town was not put on a sound basis until the eighteenth century.
This does not mean that there had been no chance to learn before
then, but we have no knowledge of any regular system earlier than
1711.

The deposition of Charles I and the period of Cromwell's
commonwealth provides the only major interruption in the life of the
town between the closing of the monastery and the arrival of the
railway in the nineteenth century. Simon Gunton, a petty canon in
1643, gives a brief description of the havoc wrought by Colonel
Richard Cromwell's soldiers. The smashing of monuments and glass
was the work of ordinary vandalism, but the destruction of the
charters and other records kept in the chapter house was a more
malicious act. What happened to the library is not known and it was
only by chance that one of the registers, known as the 'Book of

Robert of Swaffham', was saved, a soldier selling it when he was told it was some old Latin bible.

The Cromwellian Parliament abolished bishops and deans and chapters, and holders of these offices lost their houses and incomes. The town remained untouched by this, as it merely meant that a different body ran the courts and collected the rents and other dues. Within the Precincts, however, there was considerable destruction. The cloisters, chapter house and other buildings were sold to a speculator, who pulled them down and sold the building materials. The Bishop's Palace was greatly reduced in size. The residences of the church's hierarchy down to and including those of the singing men were sold, the military commander of Peterborough, Major Alexander Blake, taking the Deanery. The old story that Thorpe Hall was built out of the stone taken from the lady chapel is true, only much more from the Precincts also went into its building. A description of the Deanery carried out by the Parliamentary commissioners briefly reveals the disturbance to private lives this

Church, city, militia, fi
and citizenry celebrati
Victoria's Diamond Ju
1897

upheaval caused: the children of the widowed Dean Cosin were temporarily lodged in a fifth part of the Deanery under the care of Humfrey Austin just before Blake moved in.

The disestablishment of the episcopacy meant that there was a set of very considerable churches without a function. The Commonwealth, ever practical and pre-echoing a later government, determined that all those that the townsfolk did not want should be demolished, their materials being sold and the proceeds being devoted to charitable purposes. It is a testimony to the inner feelings of the inhabitants of cathedral cities that not one cathedral suffered this fate. In Peterborough Oliver St John, a rabid republican who fell out with Cromwell when he became Lord Protector, brought in a bill to save the cathedral by making it in effect the parish church. This was so popular in the town that the parishioners petitioned Parliament to demolish the real parish church so that the cathedral could be repaired. The lady chapel was demolished, so that the money paid for materials, bought by St John for his new home, Thorpe Hall, could pay for repairs to the cathedral.

CHAPTER SIX

Power, Politics and Railways

Although the fourteen Feoffees had few real responsibilities, they were slack in their duties: an order for them to repay moneys misappropriated by their bailiffs exists, and in 1633 a commission ordered them to pay more attention to the objects of their foundation. Being a Feoffee must have been a distinction where there were so few, and the original members obviously thought to make themselves exclusive. The regulation was that after ten had died the remaining four were to select fourteen new members and then retire. However, an inquest in 1603 discovered that the four survivors had given leases against the purposes of the foundation and that two were living nowhere near Peterborough. It took five years before they complied with the order to enfeoff new members. Another inquest in 1633 found that the Feoffees were spending money on things like a venison feast for themselves and the parishioners, and leasing properties to themselves and not paying the rent. They were thrown out and were replaced by five church-related members and nine others.

Everything worked relatively well until the Dean and Chapter were dispossessed in 1644. The Feoffees, including the royalist Sir Humfrey Orme, returned to their bad old ways, the numbers again going down to four with no replacements, and they were made to resign in 1656. Another set was chosen, but in 1659 the son of Oliver St John, Francis, and ten others were entrusted to choose twelve men to become governors, who would lease the town lands for the best rates at an annual public meeting. At the Restoration in the next year there was deadlock between the governors, who disbursed the income, and the old Feoffees who now let the lands. In 1683 the two bodies were amalgamated, their accounts to be inspected at least once a year by either the bishop or the dean, the kind of check which had not existed before.

The only visible monument to the Feoffees is the Guildhall in

Cathedral Square. There had been a covered area here called the
Butter Cross, one of the two structures on Speed's thumb-nail sketch
published in 1610. The Feoffees let out space on market days here
and had the use, apparently, of a guildhall, which they actually owned
and where they held feasts, and a moot hall where the manorial and
other courts met. The latter stood fronting the Marketstead, as the
letting of stalls under it shows, and was probably where Miss Pears'
almshouses were to be. Where the Guildhall was is unknown. The
new structure, called the Chamber over the Cross, was built by John
Lovin in 1670–1, the various coats of arms representing parties who
were interested in the town's welfare and who had provided
donations towards its building. In 1874 it became the first town hall,
the Council changing its name to the Guildhall in 1876 for no good
reason. Lovin first appears in 1642, when he was in arrears with his
rent, and again in 1659 when he was commissioned to repair the
bridge abutments. He was a local craftsman, and the 'new' style used
at Thorpe Hall, twenty years before, did not affect him.

In 1790 an Act of Parliament allowed the Feoffees, for a payment of £500, to pass responsibility for lighting and paving to a separate body of Improvement Commissioners who levied a rate and appointed watchmen, but their powers did not include the Precincts, Westgate or Boongate, the Dean and Chapter keeping responsibility for these. Another Act, of 1850, allowed ratepayers to elect new Commissioners who were now responsible for Westgate. The whole of this archaic local government edifice was swept away in 1874 when a proper Mayor and Corporation of six aldermen and eighteen councillors was elected for the first time. The Feoffees continued in charitable works until 1907 when the two almshouses in Cumbergate and the Wortley almshouses were transferred to a national trust.

The political life of the town was limited until 1874, the day-to-day affairs of manorial courts and the bodies of Feoffees, Governors and Commissioners being essentially closed shops. Parliamentary elections were few and far between and these were usually swayed

Cumbergate, almshouse, 1904

by powerful factions outside the town. The basic qualification to be an MP seems to have been the possession of a copyhold tenancy from the Dean and Chapter who, as lords of the manor, had the right to return the Members of Parliament, but it is the nature of politics that external influences aided their selection. Lord Burghley, having acquired the bishop's jurisdiction, should have been the most powerful man, yet except in the late sixteenth and early seventeenth centuries, this seems not to have been so. A later Lord Exeter tried in 1728 to get himself made the returning officer, but was thwarted.

The first MPs, returned in 1547, were Sir Wymond Carew, Treasurer of First Fruits and Tenths, and Richard Pallady, related to the Kirkhams, a locally influential family; they may both have been selected by Sir John Russell, the first Earl of Bedford and High Steward to the Dean and Chapter. The next MPs were Sir William Fitzwilliam, whose family bought Milton about 1502, and Sir Walter Mildmay, who had acquired Apethorpe in 1550, his father being one of the Commissioners who received the surrenders of other monastic houses. Sir Walter was a surveyor to the Court of Augmentations and later Chancellor of the Exchequer, and he sat for Northamptonshire for the rest of his life. A Mildmay was elected in 1572 and Edward Wymarke, who sat from 1603 to 1620, was a Mildmay man. In 1617 Francis Fane's wife inherited Apethorpe and he later became the Earl of Westmorland. Mildmay Fane was elected in 1620, 1625 and 1627 and other Fanes appear in the elections of 1660, 1661 and 1671.

The Russell family seems to have preferred to operate through nominees: their steward, Giles Isham, and John Gamlin, who was related by marriage, were returned in 1554. They also used other relationships, including the Mildmays, and these account for Thomas Hussey, elected in 1558. The Russells seem to have withdrawn from Peterborough about 1580, their leases passing to the Fitzwilliams, although there is a suspicion that the Russells' political links were with the Cecils: Sir William Cecil stood in at Peterborough when the second Earl was away in Ireland and this connection explains the appearance of Maurice Tyrell back in 1555. Similarly Nicholas Tufton of Kent (elected 1601) had married into the Cecil family. The last Cecil before the twentieth century was David, who was elected in 1640.

The Wingfields arrived in the neighbourhood in 1544 when Robert Wingfield junior, elected 1558/9, 1562/7 and 1572 and one of the Commissioners who set up the cathedral in 1541, bought Ailsworth and Upton. He married into the Cecil family showing

Wortley's workhouse of 1
altered in 1837 to form
almshouses

where his affiliations lay, especially as he was on bad terms with the
Fitzwilliams. A John Wingfield was returned in 1597 in the
Burghley interest and the family withdrew from the area in the early
seventeenth century. Other Burghley men were James Scambler,
elected 1584 and related to Bishop Scambler who had been chaplain
to Lord Burghley, Thomas Howland, elected in 1588, and another
Richard Cecil, of Wakerley, elected in 1597 and 1604.

These powerful families and their nominees were, in the sixteenth
century, intermingled with men like the bishop's chief officer, John
Mountsteven (MP in 1555), or the Dean and Chapter's High Steward
in the county, John Campanett, elected 1547, Goddard Pemberton,
elected 1601, whose wife's brother was also High Steward, and
Thomas Howland (MP in 1588). Mary I sent a circular letter to
returning officers saying that she wished MPs to be truly
representative of the place concerned and this almost certainly
explains the sudden selection of William Lively and Gilbert Bull in
1554/5. The first appears as merchant, churchwarden and juryman in
the portmanmoot of 1544, and as a Supervisor of Meres and Fens
in 1548–9. He died in 1584. The second was also a churchwarden
(1546, 1549 and 1572) and occasionally acted as attorney in the

g on the Nene in the late
·nth century

conveyancing of tenancies. The limited records suggest that Bull
was awkward, if not curmudgeonly. He was fined in 1544 and 1548
for not attending the manorial court, fined 8*d.* for not repairing
banks in the Fens in 1548 and 1578, and fined in 1560 and 1570 for
not repairing the landlords' property – forcing him to pass the lease
to his wife. From 1572 to 1589 Bull leased the common oven in the
town. He was already a baker as he had been fined in 1570 (and was
again in 1575, 1577 and 1578) for breaking the law on the sale of
bread. He refused to allow his loaves to be weighed and swore at the
queen's laws in 1575, the latter explaining the large fine of 10*s.* In
1577 he was fined for not making a common stile by Sexton Barns,
and fined the same year and in 1580 for not keeping his pigs
properly. The general lack of details for someone like Thomas Hacke
(MP from 1586 to 1587) and his son William (MP from 1592 to
1593) suggests that they were law-abiding; they also had no obvious
affiliations. Thomas, who died in 1590, was one of the fourteen
named townsfolk in the agreement drawn up with the Dean and
Chapter in 1561 when he was leasing properties in Hithegate, the
Marketstead and Priestgate, and was also one of the first Feoffees.

Others gave favours to the Feoffees and the town, obviously to ingratiate themselves: Laurence Whitacre, elected for the third time in 1628, gave £5 towards paving the Market Hill; Christopher Hatton (MP from 1624 to 1626) is mentioned in the Town Bailiff's accounts as having sent a pair of does, possibly those used in the venison feast to which the inquest of 1633 took such an exception.

The Civil War and the Commonwealth introduced some fundamental changes. The Fitzwilliams' grip momentarily slackened. The acquisition of a lease on the Dean and Chapter's estate in Longthorpe by Oliver St John and his decision to build Thorpe Hall as his principal home sounded a new note. He and four others bought all the Dean and Chapter's rights in the city in 1654 for a handsome price, including the return of the Members of Parliament, but they probably made little profit as the Dean and Chapter resumed their rights in 1660. A legal nicety prevented Oliver St John, a famous lawyer in his youth, from having to give Longthorpe back to the Dean and Chapter as well. Cromwell offered him one of the two posts of Lords Chief Justice, and he took the Court of Common Pleas; the other, the King's Bench, was the one that condemned Charles I to death. St John's prudence saved his head, but did not save him from blame, and he eventually went into exile where he died. The St John lands, including estates in Essex and Ireland, remained with his son, Francis. He and his son, also Francis, were returned to Parliament in 1656, 1659, 1678, 1679,

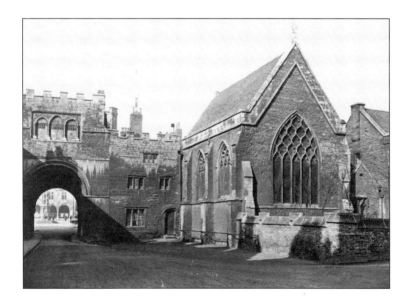

The first King's School: th Great Gate and the Chape St Thomas the Martyr, ab 1900

1680 and 1698. The estate passed to Sir Robert Bernard when the last of the male St Johns died, and on his death in 1789 the contents of the Hall were auctioned. Later, when his mother, the last St John, died, the Dean and Chapter recovered the estate, selling it in 1810 to the Earl Fitzwilliam.

The Commonwealth period was not entirely roundhead, and along with St John and Alexander Blake, the military commander of the town, the notorious cavalier Humfrey Orme, who had married a Roman Catholic, was also elected. He was a local man, his father having taken the lease of Boroughbury Manor. He was returned in 1654, 1660, 1661 and 1671. His son Charles, elected in 1679 and 1685, was often strapped for cash and took up a military career, resigning his commission when Protestant William and Mary succeeded popish James II, and this suggests that he was more than just a High Anglican.

The beginnings of party politics now appear in the form of Whigs and Tories. Often these were pejorative terms rather than marks of difference in 'policy'. Crudely, the Whigs supported William and Mary, while the Tories hankered after the good old days, without actually being traitors. Gilbert Dolben of Finedon (MP 1689–98, 1701–8), the lawyer son of an Archbishop of York and a noted Tory, provided a legal ground for formally declaring James II's reign at an end: the king, having fled, had abandoned his throne, in effect, he had abdicated. For a long stretch of the eighteenth century the two seats at Peterborough were divided between the two factions. William Brownlow, elected in 1689, 1690 and 1695, was a Whig. The Wortleys, father and son, served the city for nearly fifty years between them (1698–1710, 1722–7, 1734–61); when one was not representing Peterborough, he was probably sitting for Huntingdon. The family was actually Montagu, but Sidney took the surname of the wealthy heiress he married. The Montagus were politically important in middle Northamptonshire and Sidney's ability to afford a political life may have gained him the nomination in Peterborough, where both he and his son, Edward, sat as Whigs, although the son took an independent line on occasions.

The other side of the political coin is provided by the Tory Charles Parker (MP 1710–22) who had the lease of Boroughbury Manor. He could not stand in 1727 as he was Sheriff of Northamptonshire, so he sent the writ to the Tory Bailiff of Peterborough who returned Sir Edward O'Brien. Joseph Banks (MP 1728–34) was a Fitzwilliam man, but became a Tory, as were Charles Gounter Nicholl and Armstead Parker, the son of Charles. The 2nd Earl Fitzwilliam dealt with the Tory faction by buying the Parker lands in 1776, so turning all Parker's voters into Fitzwilliam men: as there was no secret ballot, his men knew which way to vote to preserve their tenancies. Fitzwilliam had no trouble until he tried to put in someone considered to be anti-clerical, Sir Robert Heron. Matthew Lamb (MP 1747–68) was another Fitzwilliam man who gained his seat through the influence of his uncle, Peniston Lamb, land agent to, and executor for, the 1st Earl Fitzwilliam. His grandson, William Lamb (MP 1816–19) became the Lord Melbourne who was Victoria's first prime minister.

By now the seats in the gift of great families were seldom occupied by members of the family, but rather by nominees who knew little of the local area. Matthew Wyldbore (MP 1768–80) was an exception. He was independent: the Earl Fitzwilliam counting him as favourable, but he was also marked down as a 'King's Friend', likely to vote for the government. The 2nd Earl Fitzwilliam relied upon people he knew, such as schoolfriends Henry Belasyse

Thomas Deacon's memori
the cathedral

(MP 1768–74), Richard Benyon (MP 1774–96) and Lionel Damer (MP 1786–1802), or who were 'correct' in their political views, such as French Lawrence (MP 1796–1809), or recommended, like Sir Robert Heron (MP 1819–47) and James Scarlett (MP 1819–30). The Earl's son, Viscount Fitzwilliam, continued the tradition, being a member himself very briefly (1830) and then getting John Fazakerly (MP 1830–47) elected in his place.

We have now arrived at the beginning of political parties as we understand them. Great families still wielded influence, but the direction of who was to stand in what seat came increasingly from London, the tenuous relationship between voter and his MP virtually disappearing. Some of these nominees are remembered in street names: George Whalley (MP 1852–3, 1859–78), Thomson Hankey (MP 1853–68, 1874–80) and the general political flavour of the town is represented by other streets: Cromwell, Walpole, Gladstone, Cobden, Bright and Russell. Every now and again a Fitzwilliam appears, for example G.W. Fitzwilliam (MP 1841–53) and W.J.W. Fitzwilliam (MP 1878–89), who was returned in 1885 when the city's representation was reduced to one seat. Local affection probably returned Whalley's son (MP 1880–3). From 1885 the Conservatives held the seat for eleven years, and were followed by twenty-two years of Liberal rule, until 1918 when the area of the seat increased to include the Soke. Then a period of Conservative domination set in, with the Liberals being replaced by the Labour Party. Both Sir Leonard Brassey (MP 1918–29) and Lord Burghley (MP 1931–2) were local people representing, not surprisingly, the Conservatives, but today it is customary for outsiders in every sense of the word to be nominated. All this is the stuff of history and space does not allow much in the way of biographical interest.

There were no effective local politics until 1874, but the town had not stood still in the previous seventy years. There was great commercial and industrial expansion, mainly due to the railways, which ensured that the town was no longer on the way to nowhere. In 1800 not only was none of this foreseen, but the medieval open field system round the town was still largely intact, acting as a strait-jacket on development. A private parliamentary bill culminated in an Act that brought in the Enclosure Award of 1822. The open fields were divided into blocks of land, which were allocated to individual owners according to their previous interest. For the first time agricultural land could be bought and sold, and be built on. The award map itself already shows the ground between Cowgate and Westgate, soon to be called New Town, neatly divided into small

Buckle's Brewery in New Town about 1835

parcels, and the first addition to the street plan since the twelfth century was laid out in 1827, and given the obvious name of New Road. It bypasses the whole area of Boongate. Ribbon development now became possible and this had begun by the mid-1840s. The Crescent Bridge is so called because the Crescent built in 1837 had to be demolished to make way for it. Spital Bridge records the fact that the railways destroyed what was left of the medieval Hospital of St Leonard, and the Sacristan's Grange, known by the nineteenth century as Sexton Barns, was flattened to make way for the Great Northern Railway.

The social life of Peterborough before newspapers appear in the 1850s is hard to describe, yet probably easy to determine in general terms. There was not enough genteel society to justify having an assembly room. The cathedral clergy and the attendant laity would colour life to a great degree: few card suppers and balls. That kind of frivolity was provided at Stamford. Horse racing was, however, catered for: there were meetings on Wittering Heath during most of the seventeenth century, and a racecourse at Wothorpe flourished until 1873. Musical life surely centred on the cathedral, which was the only place in the town to have an integrated musical establishment. Visiting touring theatrical companies performed where they could, but by 1774 there was a theatre next to St John the Baptist's church in the market-place. It gradually decayed and was replaced in 1846 by the Corn Hall. The location of theatres and of buildings used as such had an erratic life until the present one was opened in 1973. The only organized social body seems to have been the Peterborough Gentlemen's Society, founded in 1730. It had high ideals inspired by the Spalding Gentlemen's Society and the Society of Antiquaries of London, but became no more than a dining club. A revival in the early nineteenth century briefly admitted women, but then it became a lending library, only to disappear in 1900 when the books went to the public library.

The mists of obscurity begin to lift when directories begin to be published. These provide a convenient index of the make-up of the town. The earliest dates from 1784 and lists forty-three people, including five lawyers and two doctors. The next, in 1791, was more ambitious, listing gentry, clergy and 241 traders, including four school-teachers and two masons. The 1822/3 directory has 172 entries dealing with trade, including thirty inns, taverns and public

rough East railway
looking east before the
World War

The workmen of Thomas Moy's wagon-works about 1900

houses, and the next, for 1830, has 347 entries, including gentry: it had clearly become fashionable to be listed. The number of teaching establishments had grown to ten, and very much the same picture is presented in the 1841 directory, whose larger number of entries includes many duplications. The population had by now doubled since 1801 to 7,600; whether this was mainly due to newcomers or the natural fecundity of the natives is unknown.

This was a relatively large population and a magnet to railway companies looking for business. The first in the field was an unknown company surveying locally in 1825, but the first arrival was in 1845 in the form of a line from Northampton, offering three trains daily each way, its terminus lying south of the river. In 1847 another line opened, offering a route from the Midlands out to Boston. There followed great efforts to open a London to Edinburgh line, and the Great Northern finally opened the whole route in 1852. Peterborough became a natural centre for traffic. All three main railway companies had engine sheds here, and their workers needed housing. The first company's men lived mainly south of the river, the second company's workers lived mainly in the new housing in streets dignified with the names of great and good Liberals. The Great Northern employees lived in the 'Barracks' laid out in 1860 and now known as New England. The net result was the creation of the elongated plan of Peterborough known until after 1945, when the city and then the Development Corporation began filling in to east and west. However, in the mean time there had been a revolution in the life of the city.

CHAPTER SEVEN

The New Society

T he last sedan chair for public hire in England was in use in Peterborough as late as the 1860s, which says a lot about the character of the town before the effects of the railways were fully felt. The growing population, coupled with increasing expectations in an optimistic age, caused changes in the organization of town life and the fabric of the City. The most active form of community life in the nineteenth century centred on churches and chapels. The development of the town up the east side of the railway stretched the old parish framework of Peterborough Within and Without until the need for change was obvious. St Mark's parish along Lincoln Road was the first to be formed by an Order in Council in 1858. The parish of St Mary's, Boongate, followed in 1859, St Paul's in the north of New England in 1868, All Saints' in Park Road in 1894 and, in 1900, St Barnabas's in Taverners Road. The non-conformists in the city centre had their own chapels, the chief ones being in Priestgate (1864), Westgate (1891, replacing one of 1859) and

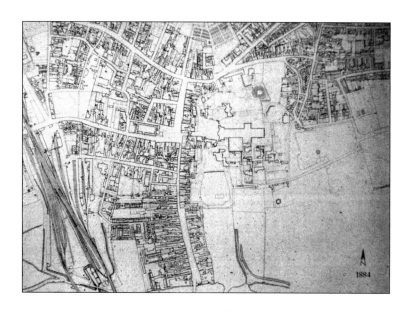

Map of Peterborough in 1884–5

in Wentworth Street (1874–5, replacing one of 1834), now demolished. The Roman Catholics built their permanent church of All Souls in Fitzwilliam Street in 1896.

The other instrument for creating the better citizen, the school, received a boost earlier. The King's School had never been intended to educate the children of the man in the street; they had to rely on charitable foundations like that founded in 1711 following a bequest of £100 by Anne Ireland. Ten years later Thomas Deacon bequeathed land and £160 a year to found a school, which still bears his name. Mrs Ireland's school survived until 1839, when the boys went to Deacon's and the girls to a church school in Bridge Street. The directories make clear there were by then many schools and teachers, and societies had come into being to spread elementary education even more widely. Although the Education Acts of 1875 and 1880 made school attendance compulsory, all education was provided on a voluntary basis until 1902 when there were eight Church of England schools, one Roman Catholic, four British and eight private schools. The City formed an Education Committee and school provision was rationalized. The Corporation had already in 1901 turned a voluntary school for the arts founded in 1883 into the School of Science, Art and Technology. A new building for it was begun in Broadway: it is still there, unfinished. From this small beginning comes the present Regional College in Park Crescent.

Education for adults in Victorian England began with a combined library and museum. The library arose from a petition in 1891 and was set up in 1893 with a gift of 2,500 books. Andrew Carnegie provided a purpose-built library in 1905, which is now next to the present Central Library, opened in 1990. The museum started in 1880 after the Corporation turned down a gift of sixty-five oil paintings and ninety-three watercolours because it refused to operate a free museum and library. The collections were run by the Peterborough Natural History and Field Club, founded in 1871, and were moved many times before going to the building in Priestgate generously given in 1931. The Museum Society ran the building and collections until 1968 when the Corporation assumed control under a deed of trust.

Among the first concerns of the new Corporation was a good water and a sewerage system. These mundane things are the very foundation of public health. The Corporation had taken over public wells from the Feoffees, four in Boongate, two in Long Causeway and one each in Westgate, Cowgate, Church Street, Bridge Street and New Town. Many had been in use for centuries and few penetrated to pure water. Surveys were undertaken to find suitable

Peterscourt, teacher-train
college, by Sir Gilbert Sc

sources and, what with these and the gaining of permission to lay pipes, it took until 1879 for the new supply to arrive. Coupled with getting water, the new Corporation strove to deal with the problem of sewerage, and this also took five years to achieve, because of powerful opposition: if important matters such as sewerage took so long to secure, the provision of a library must be seen as a triumph, even if the museum did not follow until nearly a century later.

Fire-fighting and street lighting had been old concerns: the Feoffees' accounts for 1613 itemize eighteen leather buckets, costing 3*s*. each and a further 6*s*. 5*d*. to hang them up in the parish church. The Corporation inherited the Improvement Commissioners' fire service, which had been set up in 1844. A serious fire at the Infirmary in Priestgate in 1884 revealed deficiencies and the Volunteers Fire Brigade was formed to run in tandem, as it still does. In 1822 a Mr Hallam acquired land for a gas works to provide gas lighting in the town. The company was bought in 1845 by James Sawyer, who benefited from the town's expansion after the railway had arrived as the gas mains followed the development. The first proposals for electric power were made in 1879, but a fully functioning plant on the site of Rivergate was not opened until 1900.

After education and basic utilities, public security deserves a mention. The first modern police force was set up in 1839 under, by a quirk of politics, the control of the Chief Constable in Northampton, the *only* power any county official wielded in the Soke until the late nineteenth century. The new Corporation had its own force operating within the City limits. The Norman-style jail in Thorpe Road was built in 1839 to replace both the Lord Paramount's jail, next to the Bishop's Palace, and the Dean and Chapter's jail by

erkins' factory about

the Great Gate. The jail itself closed in 1878, but the court building that survives was used until 1986.

The first public medical care was a result of the disbanding of the local volunteer cavalry at the end of the Napoleonic Wars, the residue of its funds being given to found an infirmary, which opened in 1816 in Cowgate. New accommodation was provided in 1822 by the Earl Fitzwilliam, and Squire Cooke's house, now the museum, was turned into a hospital on his death. The City never maintained a general hospital, although it set up a fever hospital on the initiative of the Medical Officer of Health. A new building was put up in 1908 at Low Farm, effectively destroying the surviving traces of the last surviving medieval grange, Boroughbury having been broken up by speculators in 1892.

All this has to do with the workings of a town, but it is the physical environment that makes the greatest impact. The bustle of the market-place has been replaced by sauntering pedestrians, the process taking a hundred years. The Ecclesiastical Commissioners, themselves inheritors of the rights of the Dean and Chapter, sold the rights to run the cattle market in 1861 to a company who moved it from the City's streets to a new site in 1863. It did not make enough money and in 1891 the market was sold to the Corporation, who also failed to make it profitable. Its site was occupied by the present market in the 1960s when that was moved out of Cathedral Square. When the City took over, the town end of Broadway was formed and so provided an extra link to the first piece of town planning seen in the City. This was laid out over 200 acres in 1876 by speculators and based on Park Road, Broadway and the great loop of Park Crescent. The park was designed to attract people to the area, and little time was lost in selling it to the new City.

One of the major changes in daily life during this period has been the way in which we spend our leisure time. Organized outdoor activities and the facilities to enjoy them are expected, but few realize how recent most of them are. Cricket and football both only got underway towards the end of Victoria's reign; even the provision of a place for the public to swim goes back to that time. The provision of public recreation spaces in towns only really took shape as planning laws and theory came to bear on the needs of a growing population and, like the twenty-year plan published in 1951, all must have seemed in place for a continued steady growth both of the town and of civic pride after the end of the Second World War. However, Dr Beeching's celebrated cuts in the railway services hit Peterborough particularly hard. The town went into an economic decline only halted by its designation as a New Town in 1968. The basis of the new town plan turned out to be the 1951 plan, which seemed to have been shelved.

'Children's Corner' in Th Park about 1910

train by Peterborough
tation, before
ng's axe fell

r comes to town, on the
of Queen Street and
te, early twentieth

The success of the Development Corporation depends on what the reader's criteria are, but there can be no doubt that the town is larger, better served as a shopping centre, cleaner and generally more pleasant than it was when the writer arrived in 1972. The City appears to be well placed to take advantage of whatever the future has to offer.

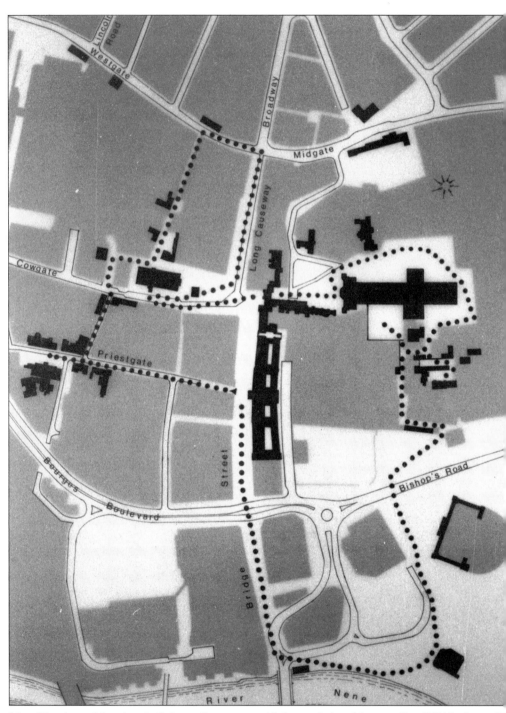

Map of Peterborough based on the Ordnance Survey maps with the permission of the controller of HM Stationery Of
Estate Publications, Crown Copyright

A Walk Through Peterborough's Past

T The walking tour is short: Peterborough was always small and its development into a busy industrial town has been accompanied by an enormous destruction of old buildings in favour of big commercial and prestigious corporate premises. The period from the late nineteenth century up to the Second World War was particularly destructive. The adoption by major companies of commercialized 'contemporary' architecture in the late 1950s led to further demolition and the disruption of scale that is so obvious when the Norwich Union Building, Barclay's Bank and Woolworth's are looked at.

The tour starts at the Town Hall, proceeds up Priestgate, the only street conveying the character of the town before the late twentieth century, to the Museum, along Cross Street and on into Queen Street, right into Exchange Street and then left into Cumbergate. The route runs through the arcade to Westgate then right along Westgate to the crossroads where the tour turns right and so on to Cathedral Square. After noting among other things the old parish church and the Guildhall, the visitor turns east and goes through the abbey's Great Gate into the Precincts. The tour deals with the cathedral's interior first, and secondly follows a route through the Precincts past the Almoner's Hall to the east gate. From there the route goes past the lido down to the river by the Theatre and then to the Customs House. Walk up Bridge Street from here, back to the Town Hall. Access for the disabled is provided throughout, including the upper floors of the Museum.

Stand opposite the Town Hall and look at its portico. The culmination of the early life of the city was the building of a town hall worthy of the aspirations of the City Council. Previously it had

had to put up with the Chamber over the Cross, with various city departments scattered about the town. A competition held in 1928 resulted in the prize and commission going to E. Berry Webber. On the whole the design is successful. As all that side of Narrow Street was demolished, there were no earlier buildings into which it had to fit. The long frontage can only be seen to advantage from each end and down Priestgate, which gives a good view of the Corinthian portico. On each side of that the central block of the building is marked by three giant windows marking the council chamber and reception hall, the mayor's parlour being behind the portico. The generally early eighteenth-century style of the exterior owes a lot to Christopher Wren's Chelsea Hospital and Hampton Court in design and also in the use of stone decorative detailing with brick. The staircase hall is well worth a glance and is in early Italian renaissance mode with rather startling blue columns and frieze, the whole recalling some of the fantasy cinemas of the 1920s and 1930s. On either side of this civic display run offices of a more mundane appearance. The top mansard storey was added in the 1980s in a different style, as changes in building regulations prevented the original design from being followed

The Town Hall portico
opposite Priestgate

Turn round and walk down Priestgate.

The Angel Hotel stood on the left until the early 1970s. The building had no great pretensions, but fitted in well with the quiet street frontages that used to lie on each side. The best surviving side is on the north towards Cross Street, but the low building painted white on the left is sixteenth and seventeenth century in appearance. This is more in the massing of the building than in any genuinely surviving parts. The gable at the south end has a sundial dated 1665, which used to look out over a garden where the telephone building now is. The building with the tower and spire was built in conjunction with the Trinity chapel in 1864, hence Trinity Street, which stood behind with its Sunday School building. Both were demolished in the 1970s. The tower and spire are commonly thought to have been inserted into an eighteenth-century building, but alas this is wishful thinking.

The Museum stands back from the road behind a line of trees and some grass. The general shape of the building derives from the private house built by Thomas, better known as Squire, Cooke,

s on the north side of
gate at the west end

which stood here and has all but gone. By the steps to the original basement is a displaced date-stone giving 1816 and his name. All that survives above this is the back wall of the eastern part of the main block. Most of what is left dates from after 1821 and represents an enlargement carried out for Squire Cooke. Conversion into a hospital and a disastrous fire towards the end of the nineteenth century have done nothing for the interior, only the entrance hall, the main corridor and the doors on either side, the stairs and the two lower rooms behind the stairs betraying any sign of the domestic grace of a large private house. Within, the Geology Gallery, the Norman Cross Room and the Archaeology Gallery are of especial note. The first has a fossil collection, the second a remarkable collection of artefacts made by French prisoners taken in the Napoleonic Wars, while the third has Iron Age swords and Roman pottery made in the Nene Valley.

Opposite the Museum can be seen various houses with eighteenth-century origins. The one with the arched door was once the vicarage of St John the Baptist's church.

> **Turn right from the Museum's front door and take the first left into Cross Street.**

Planned in the twelfth century as a link between two street frontages, there are no buildings of interest in Cross Street that belong to it alone. At the far end on the left is a Victorian public house built as the Falcon and refronted and extended in 1897. The building on the right corner is elaborately decorated and was built as a bank. Both show how buildings could be accommodated to the scale of those around, unlike the Norwich Union Building facing you, built in 1962–3 on the site of the Corn Hall of 1846, which in turn replaced the Playhouse. This stood where the Butchers' Shambles had been since at least the middle of the thirteenth century.

> **Turn slightly left and go down the left and side of the Norwich Union Building.**

On your left is a mid-eighteenth-century house of quality. This shows in the stone trim of the central Venetian window and door, the stone keystones and sills of the windows and the row of urns on the parapet. The design is enhanced by the discrete recessed panels under the first-floor windows. The interior has been 'modernized'.

> **Turn right and go down Exchange Street to the corner on your left and there turn into what is left of Cumbergate.**

Ignoring Queensgate straight ahead, this thoroughfare is one of the few places left that gives the sense of scale that belongs to a small market town. On your right is a converted terrace, part of Miss Pears' almshouses, which used to have gardens in front that had been laid out

rgate, the Still
oing renovations, late
nth century

over the cottages that formed the earlier almshouses. The earlier part of the range facing the church was put up by the Feoffees in 1835 and extended as a result of Miss Pears' will in 1903. The House of Correction used to stand here. The building with the oversailing front on the far left was also an almshouse. This is the one remaining building with a substantial medieval structure inside. Built originally as two houses, it was amalgamated into one in 1721 to form a workhouse and, when a new workhouse was built in Westgate, into an almshouse.

Go through Queensgate into a small open area.

This marks the turn of Cumbergate to Long Causeway. The building on the left was The Still and, despite its 'modern' garb, has seventeenth-century features in its structure and the remains of eighteenth-century panelling inside. The carriage way leads through to what is left of a large walled garden.

Go through the arcade, an interwar development of some attraction, to Westgate.

To your left along Westgate is Boroughbury, the town end of

Lincoln Road. The only buildings of interest along here are both on
the south side. The first is a hostelry, with an ashlar front on a
podium in which is a basement, one of the few in Peterborough
because of the high water table. The building itself is five bays wide
with decorative quoins and a string dividing the two floors, all of
whose openings have the same bolection moulding. Almost opposite
Boroughbury is a long low brown stone building of seven bays with
a large tablet over the door telling us that it was built in 1744 by
Edward Montagu MP, an example to his electorate of his
munificence. It began life as a new workhouse and; when another
was built in 1835 in Thorpe Road, was extensively remodelled in

The Arcade between
Cumbergate and Wes
pre-war enterprise

1837 by the Feoffees as an almshouse. The modernization fitted Tudoresque decoration to the pre-existing windows and central door without disturbing the original stonework very much.

Turn right down Westgate.

On your left is the Bull Hotel. The date of the building is not clear. The deep eaves along the top and the rebuilding of the top of the wall are early twentieth-century. However, a building of this size is marked on the survey of 1721 and there is nothing in the stonework to argue against a late seventeenth- or early eighteenth-century date. The size of the building, nine bays, and the upright form of the windows, obviously without ever having had mullions, suit a person of consequence: it may have been the earlier Mansion House, replaced on the right later in the eighteenth century by an imposing stone structure, whose garden was lost when Broadway was laid out in 1888, the house being demolished in about 1925.

Stop on the corner of Westgate with Long Causeway and look straight ahead.

Midgate is the short road down to the end of the building on the right; beyond that lies City Road, once Howegate. The large pinkish brick building in the middle of your view is Peterscourt, the finest surviving piece of Victorian architecture in Peterborough. Designed by Sir George Gilbert Scott as a teachers' training college and built in 1856–64, it relies on its proportions and the rhythm of windows and chimney-stacks to make its point. The more elaborate part at the far end was the principal's house, and the modern office block beyond lies on the site of the small school built to give teaching practice for the students.

The Victorian building in yellow and red brick hidden beyond the unfortunate concrete structure on the left corner was built as the County Court for the Magistrates of the Liberty or Soke in 1873, and remained in use by them until 1986.

From the corner of Westgate with Long Causeway turn right and walk to Cathedral Square.

As you walk along Long Causeway, you will see on the left a small group of some of the oldest commercial premises in the town showing above the modern ground floors. The one at the end must have been the narrowest shop in the whole town. Provincial House beyond replaced the last two eighteenth-century buildings in the street. At the end you come to the old Marketstead, which was the core of the medieval town and in many ways still is the town centre, even if its original function has gone. It is now much smaller than it was, the church along with the buildings to its west having taken up half of it. On the left lies the Great Gate into the Precincts and on the right lies the Guildhall with the church behind it. The intimate scale of the area is destroyed by the wholly inappropriate Barclay's Bank building; even the large Victorian brick and stone building on the corner with Long Causeway manages to be less offensive. The low buildings facing the entrance to the church are largely seventeenth-century, but have been severely modified.

The church of St John the Baptist was built in the first decade of the fifteenth century, the porch with the room over being added later in the century. The east end, with the exterior niches on either side of the east window, should also be part of the original church, as it was customary to begin building at this end so that services could be held as soon as possible. The gable along with all the clerestory has been rebuilt. The materials from the original church and the nave of the chapel of St Thomas the Martyr were used, but the only sign of this is the west door, the window above and, inside, the mouldings of the three arches supporting the tower, which are earlier than any other detailing now to be seen. The outer orders are twelfth-century, while the rest are thirteenth- or fourteenth-century. The arches show that the original design started out with aisles clasping the tower. Thus the size of the church was from the beginning intended to be very much as it is now, and this is confirmed by the details of the piers and arches: these are uniform from end to end, demonstrating that the present plan was also fixed. The detailing of the top of the buttresses along the aisles shows that the original parapets had been fitted with decorative battlements and pinnacles. The tower is handsome, with large belfry windows and, rising from the battlemented polygonal buttresses, crocketed spires that once echoed the lead-covered spire taken down in 1819.

The size of the church argues for a very large congregation, but much space would have been taken up by wooden benches, none of which remains. The furnishings of the chancel, along with the screens, pulpit and benches in the nave and aisles, were designed by J.L. Pearson and made by John Thompson, architect and contractor in charge of the cathedral restoration. All lend a general fifteenth-century air to the interior, which would otherwise be rather bare. The monument to Matthew Wyldbore at the east end of the south aisle is of particular note. The other monuments and grave slabs all show that Peterborough was quietly prosperous through the eighteenth century, although it is worth bearing in mind that fashion and the availability of good slate and cheap marble has much to do with this.

Next to the east end of the church stands the Guildhall. Built in 1670–1 by John Lovin for the Feoffees, as a replacement for the covered area known as the Butter Cross and dignified originally as the Chamber over the Cross, it is a single first-floor room standing on three arches front and back and two at each end, with strongly supported corners. The mullioned windows and the retrograde detailing of the building show that John Lovin learnt his trade in the earlier part of the seventeenth century and was not influenced by the then up-to-the-minute design of Thorpe Hall. Access to the upper floor used to be by a stair on the west side, and at various times buildings have been attached to that side and the north, hence the blocked doors and many rebuildings there. The name Guildhall was given in 1876 and the added buildings were the first council offices.

Turn to face the cathedral.

The Great Gate has lost a storey since it was first drawn, and the appearance was further altered when Narrow Street was widened in 1929. All the buildings on the right were removed, including one of the few imposing town houses that Peterborough ever had. The bank building is, however, a worthy replacement, its design owing more than a little to Kirby Hall. The bank on the other corner, built 1913, is undistinguished and sits on the north half of the nave and aisles of the chapel of St Thomas the Martyr. Both serve to frame the Great Gate whose façade is early fourteenth century. Abbot Godfrey de Crowland had the whole remodelled so a portcullis (note the slots on each side) could be let down in front of the gate proper. This is twelfth century and was built by Abbot Benedict. The blind arcading

The gateway to the
early sixteenth cen

on either side serves to identify his work inside the cathedral. The
vaulted rooms on the south side were once part of the abbot's prison,
later the Dean and Chapter's, and the over-restored door on the north
opened into the Porter's Lodging.

**Go through the Gate to a point about half-way to the
cathedral, and turn round.**

You are now in Galilee Court. The building on the right of the
Great Gate is a remodelling of the Porter's Lodging and next to that
is the earlier fourteenth-century chancel of the chapel of St Thomas
the Martyr. When the chapel was closed down it was converted into
the school room of the King's School and still has the earlier
nineteenth-century school fittings. The stone building to the right was

the nineteenth-century headmaster's house. The terrace of three tall houses in grey-brown brick with red brick dressings belongs to the second quarter of the eighteenth century. The podium in front is made up of six brick vaults and is an unusual feature. The nineteenth-century terrace in the corner lies on the site of the hall belonging to the monastic treasurer. Turning slightly to the right, the low stone building with Tudor detailing to the right of the exit to Wheel Yard once housed the King's Bedesmen and was remodelled in 1864. Next to that is the end of what was once the dean's coach house and stables, and the long wall from there to the gate in the corner marks the limits of the Deanery here. The gate itself is a fine example of late medieval design. It was put up by Abbot Robert Kirkton (1496–1528) as an entrance to the lodgings of, it is thought, the prior, and the thirteenth-century hall still forms the core of the building. There is a local story that says this was the entrance to the abbot's deer park, but this is patently wrong. There may be much of the Deanery described in 1649 inside the present building, but as we see it now it is the result of a major remodelling in 1842 with some later additions.

Turn to face the south side.

This range of buildings was once the offices of the abbot. It included the King's Lodging, and behind lay the Abbot's Lodgings. What is left of these forms the core of the Bishop's Palace. The chief feature is the gateway with its tower, leading to the private grounds of the bishop. Although built in the main between 1214 and 1222, the windows are much later and the jambs of the main north and south gates were rescued from its twelfth-century predecessor. The main room over the gate is known as the Knights' Chamber, probably because it housed the abbot's knights who were in attendance on him. Originally they would have been in the castle, but when that was demolished other premises were needed. The statues on both the north and south fronts are the original ones.

The range to the west of the gate was worked over last century, but the basic design reflects its seventeenth-century predecessor which almost certainly replaced the King's Lodging. The range running east from the gate is, next to the gate, mainly nineteenth-century, but the great bay window is set in an eighteenth-century building and the block at the far end is medieval, but has been heavily worked over. There used to be a building between that and

East end of the Abb
Offices, middle and
medieval, and later

the cathedral, incorporating a gate, and the remains of this can be seen on the east wall, as can the remains of an earlier vaulted chamber. Abbot Godfrey de Crowland was granted a licence to crenellate the gate to his lodgings and the buildings between that and the church in 1309.

Turn to face the cathedral.

The West End, with its Galilee Porch made up of three great arches, is the most famous aspect of the building and will be dealt with after the tour of the interior.

Go into the cathedral.

As you go through the door, notice the base of the column dividing the west door into two. This is usually said to be Simon Magus being taken by the Devil. It is more likely to be a pendant to a Doom carved in the spandrel above the double opening and under the single arch over both, showing a soul falling into hell. Unfortunately there has been no chance in modern times to look for evidence of a Doom.

the remains of the
Offices looking
n Windy Alley

The view from the west door is impressive and shows you the only great church left in England that appears to be twelfth-century from end to end. The only visual disturbances to this impression are the east and west arches of the crossing and the tracery in the windows of the apse. One of the chief features of Peterborough Cathedral is its uncluttered interior, and the clean lines of the twelfth-century design benefit from the general lack of monuments and wall tablets. Until modern times the view was never so open. The monastic layout had a screen and a stone pulpitum in the third bay of the nave from the east; this survived until about 1780 when a more 'modern' one was introduced. Blore, in about 1830, provided a new stone screen across the east side of the crossing, which was removed in the restoration works carried out from 1883 when the central tower was rebuilt. The late nineteenth-century stalls were once closed at the west end, but the wings were removed to improve the view.

> **Go to the right and walk along the south aisle (noticing the traces of medieval decorative painting in the vaults) and walk into the area under the tower.**

You are standing in the liturgical centre of the monastery and cathedral. The medieval layout survived until the early nineteenth century (even if the original stalls had been destroyed in 1643), the choir running through the area of the crossing so that the singing rose up into the lantern of the central tower. The present arrangement is neither fish, fowl nor good red herring. The great brass eagle lectern was provided by Abbot William Ramsey (1471–96).

The rebuilding of the monastic church after the fire of 1116 began in 1118 and the work carried out under Abbot John de Séez, who died in 1125, is fairly easy to distinguish. He laid out all the east end and the eastern walls of both transepts, and carried the building as far as the top of the tribune level over the main arcades. The difference between a triforium and a tribune is that the latter has external windows, thus making it a proper gallery. Abbot John was responsible for the use of the chevron or zig-zag on horizontal mouldings, and an incomplete course of this can be seen at this level, especially next to the north-east pier of the crossing. To him must be attributed the one feature that was not followed under Martin de Bec, and that was the building of aisles along the western side of the transepts, although the foundations for these were partly laid. The best way of seeing which is Abbot John's work is to look at the mouldings of the blind arcading in the aisles of the east end. There is a subtle difference from the mouldings used under Abbot Martin (1133–55), who carried on the rebuilding after the disastrous episode of Henry, Abbot of St Jean d'Angeli (1128–33), which have a small rebate round the top. Abbot Martin completed the eastern arm, or presbytery, by 1140, when he moved the monks from the patched-up old church into it. To him belonged the great arch that used to span the beginning of the apse where there is now an awkward transition in the roof. After demolishing what was left of the old church he built the transepts to the tops of the four piers of the central crossing. As far as the nave is concerned, he built the south aisle as far as the door into the cloisters, as the mouldings in the blind arcading and pier bases show. But he only laid out the first four bays on the north side to buttress the piers of the crossing, and only one bay of the aisle wall. He may not have run the south aisle into the corner of the cloisters because the lower part of the Late Saxon tower may still have been standing as a marker for the new west end.

The cathedral, the w
inside the south end
Galilee

Abbot William de Waterville (1155–75) is said to have built the three stages of the central tower, which may all have been above the great arches, the eastern one of which would have been built by Abbot Martin to complete his work. Abbot William's tower was swept away in the fourteenth century when both the early east and west arches were replaced. As you look up into the lantern to view the fourteenth-century wooden vault, all the stone in the tower, except for the slightly browner material, is the original facing, which was replaced when the whole was rebuilt from bedrock last century.

The present appearance of the presbytery belongs to the late nineteenth century, the chief features are the floor and the ciborium. The first is of *opus Alexandrinum*, a mixture of cut marble pieces (*opus sectile*) and mosaic and the second is in sumptuous marble and alabaster, tricked out with cosmati work over the high altar, all designed by J.L. Pearson, the cathedral architect in charge of the restorations. Peterborough owes much to Pearson and the skill of his Clerk of Works, J.T. Irvine, for the sympathetic treatment of the actual building: whether one likes the look of the presbytery or not, what is there rested on the taste of a committee.

The other chief feature of the presbytery is the wooden vaulting. This is fifteenth-century and is fitted with many carved roof bosses. The awkward junction with the flat ceiling over the apse could suggest that the arch here was only taken down after the vault was

inserted, but there are extensive thirteenth-century modifications to the top of the apse suggesting that it was removed then. What is certain is that until 1643 few people would have been aware of this change in the roofing because of the enormous pinnacled screen that stood in this position on the wall behind the high altar, and which is reported to have risen almost to the roof. The flat ceiling beyond was painted in the late 1850s, the design following the outline of what survived the muskets of Colonel Cromwell's rude soldiery.

Go into the south transept.

One of the three oldest stones on display inside the cathedral is built into the west wall. It shows two figures, almost certainly intended to be bishops. Although these are now weathered the quality of the original carving can be detected at the lower end. A second stone, with crisp interlacing, is built into the south-west pier of the tower and these, along with the so-called 'Monks' Stone' in the New Building, the stones at St Margaret's, Fletton, and the best preserved of all at St Cyneberga's at Castor, all date to the late eighth or early ninth century. The west wall has a door in it to what

hedral, the vaulting
orth end of the

is now the sacristy, which is not open to the public. In the twelfth-century stonework over and to the right of it, you will see the outline of the original door. The sacristy lies between the church and the cloisters, and occupies the site of the western aisle that was abandoned by Abbot Martin. The vaulting was inserted under Abbot Benedict, of whom more anon. The line of windows above the door and the capitals of the blind arcading generally contain the last stock of material prepared under Abbot John but used by Abbot Martin, although he himself had opted for a simplified decorative suite for his building programme. A careful examination of the stonework and patched-in plaster of the south wall will reveal where the night stairs from the dormitories into the church once ran down from the lower right-hand window.

The east side has an aisle divided into three chapels. These are, from the south, the chapel of St Cyneberga and St Cyneswitha, the sisters of King Wulfhere who had retired to a monastery at Castor; the chapel of St Benedict whose Rule the monks followed; and the chapel of St Oswald. This is of particular interest. Not only was the saint's arm the most important relic the monastery possessed, but the chapel itself is deliberately placed immediately east of the place in the Late Saxon church where previously the arm had been kept. On the north side can be seen the spiral staircase up to the watching gallery, from which guard was maintained over the shrine on the altar. On the other side of the wall here is an arch under which Abbots John, Martin and Andrew were buried, as close to the saint as they could be got with dignity. The screens across the entrances to these chapels have extensive traces of medieval decorative painting. The three east windows here are all the same and their design reflects what is recorded of the windows of the lady chapel; it seems highly likely that all are of the same date, basically the last quarter of the thirteenth century.

Go east along the south aisle of the presbytery.

On your right lie four effigies of abbots, some of whom have been tentatively identified. As no monument has a name on it and the bulk of these effigies fall into a narrow period, late twelfth to mid-thirteenth century, when there were eight abbots, there can be no certainty. At the far end in the New Building is the very battered effigy of John Chambers, the last abbot and first bishop.

In the last arch on your left, just before you go into the New

site: the south-east
of the crossing in the
dral before demolition
83, showing the
nth-century
gthening with timber
s and iron bands

Building, is the first burial place of Mary Queen of Scots. Her body was moved to Westminster Abbey by her son, James I and VI.

Originally there was an apse at the end of each aisle of the presbytery, and the outline of the south one is marked in the floor here. These were done away with in the thirteenth century when new square ends were built and the altars were raised up on two steps. The piscinas of the altars remain and the top of the rough work at the foot of the side walls marks the altar level in these chapels. In the north wall is a niche containing pieces from the great screen behind the medieval high altar. The east walls were taken out to provide access to what is still called the New Building. On the external wall of the twelfth-century apse on your left is Sir Humfrey Orme's monument, damaged in 1643, and beyond this is the opulent marble monument to Thomas Deacon, once surrounded by iron railings, whose will left property to educate twenty poor boys in what became known as Deacon's School. He lies there making a grand gesture to Heaven, dressed in the height of fashion in wig and square-toed shoes. The monument is signed by Robert Taylor, a noted London sculptor: this is his masterpiece.

The chief glory of the New Building is the fan vaulting. This so captures the eye that the skill with which this new square end was grafted on to a round one often goes unnoticed. The original windows in the apse had their sills cut down to provide access to the area behind the great screen, while the other windows, with their earlier fourteenth-century tracery, merely had the glass removed. The New Building was put up by Abbot Robert Kirkton (1496–1528) to house three altars in fitting style and his rebus, a church on a tun or barrel, can be detected here and there in the ornaments in the string under the windows. The vaulting is so like that of King's College Chapel at Cambridge that it is highly probable that the same master mason, John Wastell, was the designer of both.

In the central arch of the apse is the so-called 'Monks' Stone', a name derived from a spurious story intended to reflect glory on fictitious exploits of the monks of Crowland Abbey in 870, hence the date carved on one end. The form of the stone is obvious, that of a shrine, but it cannot be one as it is solid. There are six figures on each side and it is highly probable that there was once another one at each end. This makes fourteen; and if you look at the central two on the side facing you, you will see that the one on the left is a woman bearing a lily, obviously the Virgin Mary, while the figure on the right is Christ with the cross carved on the halo, and next to Him on

Opposite: the cathedral, late nineteenth-century ciborium

the right is St Peter holding up a pair of keys. In other words, here is Christ, His Mother, and the twelve apostles. The object is unique.

> **Leave the New Building to go west along the north aisle of the presbytery.**

On the left-hand side is what looks like a monument. It is a mishmash of medieval nichery and fake details carved in the eighteenth century and sometimes called the shrine of St Tibba, a kinswoman of Cyneberga and Cyneswitha. Whatever it was first built as, the niches used to be behind the burial place of Mary Queen of Scots.

In the first arch on your left in the aisle is the burial place of Catherine of Aragon, wife of Prince Arthur, the eldest son of Henry VII. On his death she married Henry VIII. On her failure, for whatever reason, to produce a male heir could be said to rest the entire modern history of England. Further along on your left is a very fine Alwalton Marble effigy assigned on stylistic grounds to Abbot Benedict, who died in 1193. On your right you will pass the only twelfth-century window left at this level in the cathedral, preserved because on the other side of the wall lay the chapel of St Thomas of Canterbury, built by Godfrey de Crowland before he became abbot in 1299. The two blocked arches of different dates on your right opened into the chapel, the windows here coming from the fifteenth-century cloisters.

> **Go into the north transept.**

Obviously a repeat of the south transept, the chief point of interest here lies in the eastern wall of what had been three chapels in the east aisle. The two northern chapels were replaced by two arches leading into the lady chapel, which was begun in 1272 and dedicated in 1290, a generation before the lady chapel at Ely, which lies in the same position. In the blocking of the arches are two more windows from the fifteenth-century cloisters. The window to the right of these one-time openings has the same design as those in the south transept and may well have matched those in the lady chapel demolished around about 1651, its stone being used in Thorpe Hall. Attached to the west side of the northern pier can be seen a small pedestal. Before the image of the Virgin and Child which stood here Prior

edral, the fan
in the New

William Paris, who built the chapel as an object of personal
devotion, was buried in 1286. The four arches of the eastern aisle are
filled with medieval screenwork, which incorporates four original
doors. Although the screens look as though they have been there for
centuries they have obviously been chopped about to fit here. They

are the major part of a screen that ran right across the nave and its
aisles in front of the medieval pulpitum; it had a door in each aisle
and a door on each side of the Altar of the Holy Cross that stood in
the nave. Behind the screens at the extreme left-hand end is a
curious double seat incorporating wooden columns which are all that
survive of the thirteenth-century stalls smashed in 1643. Two bays of
the blind arcading behind you on the west side have capitals cut for
Abbot John de Séez, but used here by Martin de Bec.

Go into the nave west of the choir stalls.

The cathedral, the w
of the nave showing
springing of the inter
vaulting

Looking west, you can see the great west window now filled with
fifteenth-century tracery like all the windows around, save for those
lighting the aisles, which date to the late thirteenth century. The
tendency through the Middle Ages was always towards more light.
The twelfth-century windows were relatively small and would have
been filled with glass as dark as that to be seen at Chartres. The
stained and painted glass of the later thirteenth century was paler,
and that of the fifteenth century relied much upon golden tints.
There is no reason, however, to think that all windows in the church
would necessarily have been filled with glowing colours.

The nave ceiling is justly famous. It is the oldest of its kind and dates
from around 1200. What may not be appreciated is that it is a temporary
ceiling, as the intention was to cover the nave with vaulting. The curious
pointed arches around the clerestory windows were to seat the
stonework filling the panels formed by stone ribs. The proof that this
was to be the scheme lies in the springing of the diagonal vaulting ribs
on either side of the arch at the west end. The nave was completed for
the most part by Abbot Benedict (1177–93) who also built the pulpitum
marking the west end of the choir. He is said to have completed the
church 'up to the front', but there is some doubt as to which front this is.
The mouldings of the blind-arcading in the north aisle and at the west
end of the south show his work, for they are repeated in the Great Gate
which he is known to have rebuilt. There are two west fronts, however –
the one that is there now, and the one that was started and traces of
which only the most discerning visitor will spot unaided.

The third pier from the west on each side of the nave is fatter than
any other, the outer wall in the second bay on each side is thicker
than any other and, in the tribune on the south, if you peer at the

The cathedral, rema
the unfinished towe
first west front

right angle from the north-west, you will see the beginning of an arch running away to the south. What these features show is that there was to be a tower here on each side, and the southern one was certainly built up to the beginning of the third storey at least. If you look carefully at the walling of the left-hand part of the second pier on the south, from the bottom right up to the mouldings under the clerestory, you will see the disruption in the stonework caused when the unfinished west wall of the nave was removed when the nave was lengthened. All the detailing in the bays west of the intended towers up to the western transepts belongs to Abbot Benedict and the bases match the central section of the north arcade of the nave, but he did not live to see it finished. He is said to have begun 'that marvellous work next to the brewery' and it is almost certainly the lower parts of the western transepts that were meant.

The western transepts are a mixture of later twelfth- and earlier thirteenth-century work. If you look at the great windows at the ends of the western transepts, you will see that the east side is twelfth-century and the west thirteenth, while the walling above is twelfth again. The main arches across the western transepts are very close to 1200; notice their zig-zag mouldings. Notice also the great circular holes, which were to allow bells to be hoisted into belfries planned for them. A detailed analysis of the whole of the west end has yet to be undertaken, but it looks as though there are two major stages and two minor ones in its completion. Before you leave the cathedral, note the very fine Alwalton Marble font at the north end of the western transepts and the mural painting to Old Scarlet. The impressive wooden leaves of the three doors at the west end all date from before 1238, when the monastic church was dedicated in a major ceremonial marking the official end to building.

Go through the west door and turn to gain a good view of the west front.

What you see are three great arches with three gables over between two solid but narrow blocks of masonry, or short towers, each crowned with short spires of different dates. It is generally agreed that the original design of the frontage had the present central arch flanked by narrow ones scarcely wider than the side doorways. Each door would have had a single large window above, and part of

the mouldings of the southern one survive in a trimmed-back state. Why the decision was taken to widen these side arches is not known, nor just how much of them was built, but it is possible that enough was put up to show that the interior of the church would have become impossibly dark, even with widened windows at the end of the western transepts. The result was that the central arch became narrower than the others, an architectural solecism.

J.T. Irvine was the first to spot that there is an anomaly in the

The cathedral, the wes front

gables, and the way in which the left-hand pier leans forward is obvious to all. The reason why it leans was found when the west front was underpinned in the 1890s: the pier was sinking into the soft fill of a Roman well. Some attempts were made to correct the lean as the west front was being built, but the biggest change came when it was decided to lower the gables to save weight. If you look at the line of arches in which windows alternate with statues, just above the great arches of the Galilee, you will see that they are clumsily chopped by the slope of the gables. Furthermore, if you look at the circular windows, you can see how they cut down into the same arches that had been intended to run as a band right across the front. In fact all the decorative details are jammed uncomfortably into a small space, caused by lowering the tops, and therefore the sides, of the gables.

You will have noticed the circular holes for bells in the vaults of the western transepts inside the cathedral. These show that the idea of a two-towered front had not been abandoned, but in the event only the northern one was finished, by Abbot Richard de London

incts, part of the
y, thirteenth
with additions

before 1274, while he was sacristan. Whether he was responsible for the extraordinary lead-covered timber spire shown on the earliest prints is less certain. The last additions to the front were the fourteenth-century spires on either side, that on the south side being of a more sophisticated design than the other and seeming to incorporate parts of thirteenth-century corner pinnacles which are absent from the northern spire arrangement. The central porch is always given to the latter part of the century and shows the radical change from the earlier style to Perpendicular. The upper level of the porch is known as the Trinity chapel, and its altar should have been in front of the Judgement scene which was probably once to be seen over the double west door. The size of the west front makes the chapel look small, yet when it was fitted out as the cathedral library there was ample room for a gallery around the walls.

Now walk along the north side of the cathedral.

This was part of the monks' cemetery and became the town cemetery in 1407. Over the wall to the left is the dean's garden including at its foot the mound of Abbot Torold's castle, which lies athwart the burh wall. The twelfth-century doorway in the north wall of the nave was used in funeral processions. The heightening of the tribune in the nave shows well: the new windows, about a generation later than the ones below, are set in new walling above the twelfth-century ones.

Go beyond the north transept, with its fine Romanesque façade, and turn to look into the angle of the transept and the presbytery.

From here you can see all that is left of the lady chapel attached to the transept itself, which here has the only twelfth-century tribune windows left, and the chapel of St Thomas of Canterbury against the presbytery.

Walk round the New Building.

This takes you through an extension to the monks' cemetery given by Robert de Lindsey (1214–22) out of his vineyard. This ran all the

cincts, part of the
ry, south side,
n the late Middle

way down the east side of the Precincts when it was laid out by
Martin de Bec after 1145, but gifts of ground from it to the infirmary
by later abbots greatly reduced its size.

**Face south and look through the gate at the east end of the
south wall.**

Here you will find the thirteenth-century Infirmarer's Hall, now a
private house, consisting of a hall on the right with a chamber block

on the left, the openings here having been restored. This is the best preserved of the five medieval hall buildings left in the Precincts.

The view of the east end of the cathedral is particularly rewarding, the thirteenth-century parapet round the apse contrasting with the fourteenth-century style used everywhere else.

Turn back to look at the cathedral.

Straight ahead you can see the north arcade of the infirmary built between 1250 and 1262 by Abbot John de Caux. Its detailing, where well preserved, is very fine: look at the corbels against the west wall.

Turn west along the path and follow it round to the south.

Originally it was an aisled hall with a single pitched roof, with the aisle windows rising into gables that can be seen on the north side. The nave is now open to the skies, with a garden in front of what is left of the west wall and a roadway on the east round to Norman Hall. This end of the infirmary once opened into the chapel of St Lawrence and the blocked arch can be seen beyond the wall here. The infilled south aisle is where most of the singing men had their lodgings. The nave survived with its roof until about 1650 when it was sold for profit. The north aisle used to be housing as well, but has been reduced to two small blocks.

Go round the east end to look at the south wall.

This shows that by the end of the medieval period this part had been divided into individual rooms fitted with fire-places, making it very easy to convert into lodgings after 1541. The building to the south is Archdeaconry House and contains the remains of a mid-thirteenth-century hall as the two large windows show. In Norman Hall to the west is a twelfth-century kitchen, almost certainly the one built by William de Waterville (1155–75) for his new infirmary, which also had a cloister.

Retrace your steps to the north side of the later infirmary. Turn left, then right and go into the cloisters.

isters, the thirteenth-
doorway into the
ry

Apart from the cathedral and the sacristy in the north-east corner, building work covering four centuries can be seen. The original monastic church damaged by the fire of 1116 lies mainly under the northern part of the cloisters. The twelfth-century cloisters have gone, but the wall of the cathedral has, below the aisle windows, pairs of holes that once housed the roof timbers. In the south end of the west wall is ashlar work belonging to Abbot Ernulf (1107–14), and this is as far as he got in rebuilding the west range, his work running up to rougher earlier walling whose date has yet to be

The cloisters, a bay of
fifteenth-century lava

established. The refectory was rebuilt inside the south end of the
earlier cloisters between 1233 and 1245, which meant that a new
south walk for the cloisters was needed. The arches belonging to it
run along the east half of the wall. The new door to the refectory was
matched by a facing one into the monastic church. The cloisters
were completely rebuilt in the fifteenth century, and it is the remains
of the arches and vaulting of this that can be seen on the west side,
the other half of the south wall and on the sacristy's wall. The north
side has left no trace as it was a skin built up against the cathedral.
Of the five fifteenth-century bays along the west half of the south

hedral, the 'Canons'
in the cloisters

wall, three housed basins for the monks to wash their hands before going into the refectory, and the other two were for towel cupboards. The lower back walls of the five recesses belong to the thirteenth-century predecessor of this lavatorium.

Apart from the south transept and sacristy, the east side is now post-medieval. The solitary building here is Laurel House, named

The cloisters, 'Laurel Court', seventeenth–nineteenth century

after Laurel Court, the old name for the cloister garth. The core of the house is seventeenth-century, it being remodelled in the eighteenth. To the left of the house stood the chapter house, which was separated from the monastic church by a vaulted passage called the slype which ran through to the monks' cemetery. If you look at the corner of the transept by the head of the lowest window in the end wall, you will see a series of sockets and a ledge used to seat the joists of the flat leaded roof of the corridor from the dormitories to a door where the window now is. Although we know that the chapter house was finished before the end of the eleventh century we know nothing of it, and there is a suspicion that it had been rebuilt at least once more before Cromwell's commissioners sold it for its building materials in 1650. In the middle of the cloisters is St Chad's well, so named as a result of a concocted

story involving two sons of King Wulfhere, which was depicted in the painted glass of the cloisters, smashed in 1643.

Return to the doorway in the south-east corner of the cloisters.

This stands at the north end of a passage that once ran between the dormitory on the left and the refectory on the right, and the first five vaulting arches here are attached to its east wall. The next nine bays are fourteenth-century in date. The first six had glazed windows that once looked into a small garden, while the next housed a doorway opening into a small cloister leading to a door into the lower part of the little dorter, or dormitory. The last two bays ran between the two dormitories to a lane going in one direction to the east gates and in another to the infirmary off to your left. The dormitories were on the first floor, the smaller one running east–west, so the passages would have had an upper level, and a small trace of the door into the little dorter survives above the vaulted remains behind the last two bays on the right.

Follow the path to the south and turn left at the bottom.

The long building on your right was the Almoner's Hall built about 1400. It is divided into three main sections with an added room at the west end. Starting at the east end, the doorway with the wooden arched top once stood at the head of an external stair and was the entrance to the almoner's chamber where he kept his accounts and sometimes entertained local notables to dinner. There was also a bedroom and a corridor leading to a garderobe. Under all this were two store rooms, each with a door and a window all of which had wooden lintels. All other windows were ones of 'quality' dressed in ashlar and usually with mullions. West of the chamber block lies the Almoner's Hall proper. Here he received rents and gave orders to his tenants and officers. Because there was no internal access from the chamber block, everyone had to enter the hall through the arched door. This opened into the screens passage, which was lit by a small window at the far end. The screen stood on the left and would have had two doors into the hall itself. On the right were three doors. The hall in this phase had a central fire, two high windows, which are still there on the south and, to mark the important

end of the hall, a large single window divided into two lights and fitted with tracery in the far left-hand wall. The small niche on the left was for a night light when the fire had a curfew placed over it.

Of the three doors behind the screen at the west end of the hall, the north and south ones led into the buttery and bakehouse respectively. The buttery occupied most of the ground floor next to the hall. The central door of the three was narrow and would have opened on to steep stairs to sleeping accommodation over the buttery. The bakehouse lay at the end of a narrow corridor along the south side and occupied the rest of the original building to the west. The north wall has been completely rebuilt, but the windows in the south wall are largely original.

The room added to the west wall of the bakehouse belongs to the next major period, when the whole block was converted into lodgings for a petty canon. A door was knocked through the base of the

The Precincts, blocked windows by the path running south from the cloisters

garderobe and a staircase was run up into the corridor leading to that in the chamber block. Half of the elaborate two-light window was moved to the other side of a great fireplace inserted into the north wall of the hall. The Commonwealth profiteers seem to have divided the whole into three or four cottages and from then on it gradually deteriorated until it was rescued in 1989 to become the visitors' centre. The early surveys of Peterborough show that there were two gates across this alley, one known in the sixteenth century as Almoner's Gate and standing at the east end of the Almoner's Hall; the other, the Bull Dyke gate, lay further east, its remains lying in the Precinct wall there.

Pass through the gate and turn to the right.

Here are the Bishop's Road Gardens, opened in 1896 and still maintained in fine nineteenth-century style. The Henry Pearson Gates Memorial was transferred here from the old market-place in the 1960s and commemorates the first mayor of Peterborough. Pearson had served as the High Bailiff of the Dean and Chapter from 1857 to his retirement in 1871, and was also mayor in 1875, 1876, 1887 and 1897.

Cross over the road and walk down to the river.

Until the dumping of corporation rubbish raised the area, the whole of the ground from the gardens down to the river was liable to flooding, but now it is a public park with a tree-lined embankment. The open-air swimming pool was opened in 1936 as an act of faith in the English climate. Down by the river is the Key Theatre, and further to the east lie the Regional Swimming Pool and the stadium. At the end of Bridge Street down by the river is the stone Customs House with ashlar trimmed quoins and a cupola. The date is indeterminate but is probably earlier eighteenth-century. This is the last surviving trace of Peterborough's status as a port, which was finally strangled by the obdurate refusal of the Duke of Bedford to dredge the river further east.

From here you can walk back up Bridge Street to where you started.

The Next Steps

The following buildings in or near Peterborough are normally open to the public, although the hours may need to be checked. The Information Centre in the Town Hall should be able to provide up-to-date details. Churches can be unpredictable when it comes to finding them open. Locally, St John the Baptist's, Barnack, and St Kynebergha's, Castor, are always open; in other instances there may be notices to say where the key is kept.

The cathedral is open daily, donations are welcome and visitors are welcome to join the services, which are held at least twice daily.

The parish church of St John the Baptist in Cathedral Square is also usually open daily.

The Museum in Priestgate is, given staffing levels, open five days a week, Sunday and Monday being the exceptions, from 10 a.m. to 5 p.m.

In Longthorpe, the parish church of St John the Baptist is worth visiting along with Longthorpe Tower, which is managed by the state and is usually open. Thorpe Hall is open intermittently, but a telephone call may establish that the casual visitor can see some of the principal rooms.

All Saints', Paston, and St John the Baptist's, Werrington are perhaps more accessible than St Judith's, Sutton, or St John the Baptist's, Upton. North of the city, Marham St Mary's is worth a visit and in the south so are St Margaret's, Fletton, and St John the Baptist's, Stanground.

The best place to pursue local history is undoubtedly the Local History section of the Central Library in Broadway. Thereafter, the major records are kept in the Northampton Record Office, a relic of the days before the old county was split.

The starting point in reading about Peterborough and its immediate neighbourhood must be the *Victoria County History*, Northamptonshire Volume 2, as on the whole the local area is very poorly served with general histories. The translation of Hugh Candidus published by the Peterborough Museum Society is one of the most valuable sources for the late Saxon and early Medieval periods. Then come the volumes published by the Northamptonshire Record Society, of which the introductions to the following are essential reading:

Brooke, C.N.L. and Postan, M.M., (XX) *Carte Nativorum, a Peterborough Abbey Cartulary of the fourteenth century.*

Mellows, W.T., (IX) *Peterborough Local Administration, Parochial Government before the Reformation, Churchwardens' Accounts, 1467–1573, with Supplementary Documents, 1107–48* (1939).

Mellows, W.T., (X) *Peterborough Local Administration, Parochial Government from the Reformation to the Revolution, 1541–1689* (1937).

Mellows. W.T., (XII) *Peterborough Local Administration, the Last Days of Peterborough Monastery*, Part I of Tudor Documents (1947).

Mellows, W.T., (XIII) *Peterborough Local Administration, the Foundation of Peterborough Cathedral, A.D.1541*, Part II of Tudor Documents (1941).

Mellows, W.T., (XVI) *The Book of William Morton, Almoner of Peterborough Monastery, 1448–1467* (1954).

Mellows, W.T. and Giffard, D.H., (XVIII) *Peterborough Local Administration, Elizabethan Peterborough, The Dean and Chapter as Lords of the City*, Part III of Tudor Documents (1956).

There are many pamphlets and booklets in the Local History Collection in the Central Library dealing with all aspects of life in the city, but there are really only three other books which can be recommended, the first being more of a curiosity than the other two: Simon Gunton, *The History of the Church of Peterburgh* (1686, reprinted 1990); H.F. Tebbs, *Peterborough* (1979); M.J. Barcroft, *Luckiest of All*. Finally, the introductory sections of D.F. Mackreth, *Excavations in Peterborough, 1972–82*, forthcoming.

Acknowledgements

I give my thanks to the following for generous help: Tim Halliday, Richard Hillier, the Northamptonshire Record Office and the Planning Department of the City of Peterborough. I also give my thanks posthumously to H.F. Tebbs who introduced me to the peculiar flavour of the town. I am grateful to Mr Rex Wilcox who provided all the photographic prints as well as advice on the ones dating back to before 1960. My wife, Christine, is owed much principally for providing the necessary goal and for giving a final lay person's view of the text. Whatever offends is my own fault. Lastly my gratitude goes to David Buxton and Simon Fletcher of Alan Sutton Publishing.

Picture Credits

The author gratefully acknowledges the following for permission to reproduce illustrations: Drawing, Edward Curry; photograph, R. Wilcox: (page nos) 2, 3; engraving from E.T. Artis' *Durobrivae . . .* (1828); photograph, R. Wilcox: 4; Calum Rollo: 7; photograph, R. Wilcox from an original by A. Challands: 8, 9; drawing by J.T. Irvine; photograph, R. Wilcox from an original by D.F. Mackreth: 11, 92; drawing, Edward Curry; photograph, R. Wilcox from an original by D.F. Mackreth: 12, 16; photograph, R. Wilcox from original by Calum Rollo: 14; R. Wilcox: 17, 26, 27, 28, 32, 36, 37, 41, 42, 45, 47, 48, 54, 58, 61, 62, 67, 68, 73, 74, 75, 80; drawing, D.F. Mackreth; photograph, R. Wilcox from an original by D.F. Mackreth: 19, 44, 70; drawing, R. Colley, 1829, in author's collection; photograph, R. Wilcox from an original by A. Challands: 25; drawing, Allport; photograph, R. Wilcox: 66. All other illustrations were supplied by the author.

Index